The Way
Walking in the Footsteps of Jesus
Expanded Paperback Edition

The Way
Walking in the Footsteps of Jesus

The Way
978-1-5018-2878-2
978-1-4267-6488-2 *eBook*
978-1-4267-6733-3 *CD Audiobook*
978-1-5018-3606-0 *Large Print*
Audiobook also available from Audible.

The Way: Leader Guide
978-1-4267-5395-4

The Way: DVD
978-1-4267-5253-7

The Way: 40 Days of Reflection
978-1-4267-5252-0
978-1-4267-6490-5 *eBook*

The Way: Youth Study Edition
978-1-4267-5254-4
978-1-4267-6492-9 *eBook*

The Way: Children's Leader
978-1-4267-5255-1

For more information, visit www.AdamHamilton.org.

Also by Adam Hamilton

24 Hours That Changed the World
Christianity and World Religions
Christianity's Family Tree
Confronting the Controversies
Creed
Enough
Final Words from the Cross
Forgiveness
Half Truths
John
Leading Beyond the Walls
Love to Stay
Making Sense of the Bible
Not a Silent Night
Revival
Seeing Gray in a
    World of Black and White
Selling Swimsuits in the Arctic
Speaking Well
The Call
The Journey
Unleashing the Word
When Christians Get It Wrong
Why?

ADAM HAMILTON

The Way
Walking in the Footsteps of Jesus
Expanded Paperback Edition

Abingdon Press
Nashville

The Way:
Walking in the Footsteps of Jesus
Expanded Paperback Edition

This book is printed on elemental chlorine-free paper.

ISBN 978-1-5018-2878-2

Photos by Rob Webster. Additional photography by Mike Collins and Adam Hamilton.

16 17 18 19 20 21 22 23 24 25 — 10 9 8 7 6 5 4 3 2 1

MANUFACTURED IN THE UNITED STATES OF AMERICA.

To my father-in-law, Richard Bandy,
a remarkable man whose encouragement and support
have been such an important part of my life's journey

Contents

Preface

We have been on a journey with Jesus.

In previous volumes I explored the stories surrounding the birth of Jesus (*The Journey: Walking the Road to Bethlehem*) and those surrounding his death and resurrection (*24 Hours That Changed the World*).

In *The Way: Walking in the Footsteps of Jesus*, I will focus on the life and teachings of Jesus. As with the previous two books, I will try to help you hear familiar stories with fresh ears by drawing upon insights from history, archaeology, and the geography of the Holy Land. This book was outlined as I retraced the footsteps of Jesus across Israel and Palestine.

To supplement this book and transport you on the journey, a video is available in which I take you to the Holy Land, to the places described in each chapter. By means of the video you will travel with me to the Jordan River, where Jesus likely was baptized, and to the Judean wilderness, where he was tempted. We'll walk among the ruins of Capernaum, where Jesus made his home during his three years of public ministry. We'll climb

the mountain where Jesus may have given his most famous sermon. We'll take a boat onto the Sea of Galilee. I'll introduce you
to a Samaritan priest, one of only a handful still living. And I'll
show you Jacob's Well, where Jesus offered an outcast a drink
of living water. Finally, we'll recall the last week of Jesus' life in
Jerusalem, where these events occurred.

I've also written a forty-day devotional book that will offer
daily readings from the Gospels and brief reflections on their
meaning for our lives today, titled *The Way: 40 Days of Reflection*.

We hope that this journey, walking in the footsteps of Jesus,
will deepen your understanding of Jesus' life, while at the same
time deepening your faith in him and your love for him.

The Way
Walking in the Footsteps of Jesus

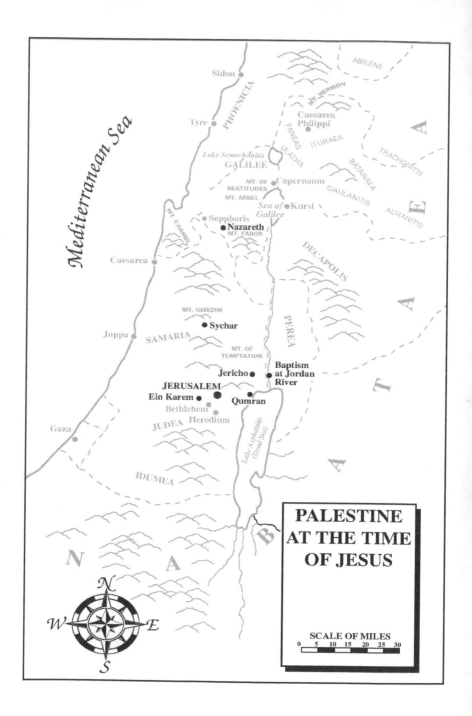

PALESTINE AT THE TIME OF JESUS

SCALE OF MILES
0 5 10 15 20 25 30

Prologue
John the Baptist and Jesus

The beginning of the good news of Jesus Christ, the Son of God. As it is written in the prophet Isaiah: "See, I am sending my messenger ahead of you, who will prepare your way; the voice of one crying out in the wilderness: 'Prepare the way of the Lord, make his paths straight.'" John the baptizer appeared in the wilderness, proclaiming a baptism of repentance for the forgiveness of sins. And people from the whole Judean countryside and all the people of Jerusalem were going out to him, and were baptized by him in the river Jordan, confessing their sins. Now John was clothed with camel's hair, with a leather belt around his waist, and he ate locusts and wild honey. He proclaimed, "The one who is more powerful than I is coming after me; I am not worthy to stoop down and untie the thong of his sandals."

Mark 1:1-7 NRSV

BEFORE WE TURN TO THE STORY of Jesus, we begin
where the Gospels begin, with John the Baptist and with a bit
of speculation about his relationship with Jesus before the day
when Jesus came to be baptized. The story begins when Jesus
and John were just boys.

Jesus went with his parents to Jerusalem every year for the
festival of the Passover. We know about these trips to Jerusalem
because of the only story in the Bible that recounts any event from
Jesus' childhood after his infancy.[1] It is found in Luke 2:39-52.

It seems that on one of these yearly trips, Jesus' parents
likely joined a caravan of friends and family to return to Nazareth,
nine or ten days' journey to the north. A day into the trip, Mary
and Joseph realized they had inadvertently left Jesus back in
Jerusalem. They journeyed another day back and searched for
him. Finally, on the third day, they found the twelve-year-old
Jesus in the Temple courts. We can feel their agitation with him
as we read the story. What parents can't identify with them and
take a bit of comfort from the fact that the Virgin Mary and Saint
Joseph had misplaced the Son of God?

The yearly Passover festival was a joyous occasion and
lasted for a week, with some Jews arriving early or staying late.
Where would Mary, Joseph, and Jesus have stayed each year as
they visited Jerusalem? It is likely they would have stayed with
their closest of kin.

Just outside Jerusalem was a town called Ein Karem.
Tradition says it was the hometown of Elizabeth, Zechariah,
and their son John, the second boy in our story, whom we know
today as "The Baptizer," or John the Baptist.

You may recall that when Mary discovered she was pregnant,
she immediately left Nazareth and traveled for nine days to the
home of Elizabeth to tell her the news. Clearly Elizabeth was an
important person in Mary's life. The Gospel of Luke calls her

simply a relative, perhaps an aunt or older cousin. Mary went on to spend the first three months of her pregnancy helping her kinswoman Elizabeth, who was in her final three months preparing to give birth to John.

John and Jesus were cousins, born six months apart, with mothers who were very close. It seems plausible that the two boys spent at least a week together each year during the Passover festival when they were small children. They no doubt played together, laughed together, and dreamed together.

Luke tells us that John went on to live in the wilderness or desert of Judea. We don't know how old he was when this happened. Some have presumed that he left when his parents died, others that Elizabeth dedicated her son to God and left him to be raised among the monks in the monastery at Qumran. How old was John when this occurred? In the absence of information, and in light of the close connection between Jesus and John the Baptist, I suggest this may have occurred when John was around the age of fourteen, when it would have been time to consider marriage.

John the Baptist and the Essenes

Luke tells us that John was "in the wilderness until the day he appeared publicly to Israel" (Luke 1:80 NRSV). Many have speculated that he went to live in a monastic community along the northwestern shores of the Dead Sea called Qumran. We believe the monks who lived there were part of a sect called Essenes. This is the community believed to have produced and hidden the Dead Sea Scrolls.

At Qumran, John would have devoted himself to God, committed to celibacy, perhaps worked in the community garden or prepared pottery, and studied and copied the Scriptures. Among

the practices of this community was ritual bathing for purification. This was a common practice among Jews in the first
century, but for the Essenes it was a daily practice that served
as a sign of their desire for purification and grace, and of God's
offering it to them. The Essenes hoped that by their pursuit of
holy living, they could usher in the coming of the Messiah.

Qumran and the surrounding region is a dry, desolate area,
flat as you approach the Dead Sea and in other areas marked
by dry creek beds called *wadis* and amazing ravines and valleys
carved into the mountains. Visiting the ruins of Qumran, you
can see multiple baptistries called *mikva'ot* (singular: *mikveh*, or
mikvah) that were used for rites of purification. There is the kiln
where pottery was made, as well as the treasury and the room
where it is believed the scrolls were copied. As you walk among
the ruins, it is possible that you are walking where John walked,
through the community where he lived for more than ten years.

To the west of the community, in the mountains, you can see
caves, dozens of them. Around A.D. 68, almost forty years after
the death of John, the Romans sent troops to the region around
the Dead Sea. During this time, the monks at Qumran hid hundreds of scrolls— copies of the various books of the Bible and
other important works—in jars and then placed them in these
caves. Two years later, Rome destroyed Jerusalem. None of the
monks, who likely had fled to Masada during this time, lived to
return and retrieve their scrolls. The scrolls were rediscovered
by a shepherd boy, whose goat ran into one of the caves 1,878
years later! I've seen some of the Dead Sea Scrolls on exhibit,
and I can't help but wonder if any of the scrolls were copied by
John the Baptist.

I'd like to suggest that after John went to live in the
wilderness, he and Jesus continued to be companions. Each
shared in common a miraculous birth, a sacred mission from

God, and a desire to call people to be part of God's kingdom. They were six months apart in age. There was no one who would have shared more in common with Jesus than John, and likewise John with Jesus. It seems likely to me that they would have continued to meet annually in Jerusalem for the Passover (there was an Essene community there) and perhaps at Qumran.

There is a strong connection between the message of Jesus and the teachings of the Essenes. One source has documented sixty-one parallels and commonalities between Jesus' teachings and those of the Essenes.[2] When we see the connections between John and Jesus, the obvious awareness of each other's ministry, the way they spoke of one another, the message they shared, and the fact that Jesus came from Nazareth to be baptized by John, it seems likely that throughout their twenties these two men spent time, as they had as boys, dreaming about and discussing together the kingdom of God.

The Jordan River, the Prophet Elijah, and John

Around the age of thirty, it appears that John decided to leave the monastery.[3] He would go to the common people and call them to repent and seek to follow God as their King. He would prepare the way for the Messiah, the promised King who would usher in God's kingdom on earth. John believed the Messiah to be his younger cousin, Jesus.

The distance from the monastery to Jericho is only about six miles, but it is a two-hour walk, and you'd better bring water because the region is a hot, dry desert. It seems likely that John first began his work in Jericho, calling people to repent. After he had begun to have an impact in Jericho, he moved his ministry to the Jordan River, just a few miles to the east, where he would baptize them. It was in this very place that the children of Israel crossed the Jordan and entered the Promised Land.

To understand the ministries of John the Baptist and Jesus, it is important to pause and recognize their connection with Elijah, Israel's great prophet of the ninth century B.C. Elijah was known for standing up against the idolatry of King Ahab and Queen Jezebel. Like Jesus, he fasted forty days and forty nights. Like John, he spent time with God in the desert. Elijah spent his last days in Jericho, then he crossed the Jordan at the place where John would baptize. On the other side, he was taken up to heaven in a chariot of fire. In the Old Testament period Elijah became the type of an idealized prophet, just as David was the type of an idealized king.

The final two verses of the Old Testament are Malachi 4:5-6: "Lo, I will send you the prophet Elijah before the great and terrible day of the LORD comes. He will turn the hearts of parents to their children and the hearts of children to their parents, so that I will not come and strike the land with a curse" (NRSV). There are several references to this verse in the Gospels as various people clearly were anticipating an Elijah-like figure to preach and prophesy just prior to the coming of the Messiah. John the Baptist was familiar with these verses and the role of the Elijah-figure in announcing the Messiah's coming.

When John preached and baptized in the Jordan, he came wearing unusual garb. Seldom do we read in the Bible about clothing, but in John's case Matthew tells us he was wearing camel's hair and a leather belt. Most people wore cotton or wool, so we know that John didn't haphazardly clothe himself this way. Rather, he chose to wear these clothes. Why? Because, as we read in 2 Kings 1:8, they were the same clothes Elijah wore. John wanted to make clear that he was playing the role of Elijah, preparing the way for the Messiah, whom he believed was Jesus.

John also saw himself as the herald in Isaiah who would shout in the wilderness, "Prepare the way of the Lord. Make his paths straight" (Mark 1:3 NRSV).

Elijah left this world at the Jordan River; John began his public ministry there. John was offering a sign, setting in motion the coming of the Messiah. Matthew, Mark, Luke, and even John begin their Gospels with the story of John the Baptist. He was a tremendously important figure whose significance is often lost on modern Christians. He came as the forerunner, preparing the way for Jesus.

Baptism

Why did John ask people to wade into the Jordan River with him to be baptized? What did this act mean to his hearers?

The idea of using water as a sign of one's desire for cleansing and of God's work in forgiving was not new to John's hearers. The Law of Moses prescribed the regular use of water for this purpose—sometimes through immersion in it and sometimes through the sprinkling or pouring of it onto the heads of those being purified. (Today Christians practice these two methods of baptism, immersion and sprinkling, and both are rooted in the Hebrew Bible.)

By the first century, special baths were used by Jews throughout the Holy Land for cleansing after childbirth, menses, or sex, as well as before entering the Temple courts. This washing was not simply a bath to clean the dirt off the body, though it could accomplish this; it was a means of expressing a desire to be clean before God and a way of experiencing the cleansing and wholeness that come from God.

As previously mentioned, the actual bath itself is called, in Hebrew, a *mikveh* or *mikvah* (plural: *mikva'ot*). Such baths have been found all over the Holy Land, many dating back to the time of Christ and before. Washing in these baths is the pre-Christian origin of the Christian baptism. Often the baths have two sets of stairs entering the water: in one set of stairs, unclean; out another set of stairs, ritually clean. This form of baptism was also used when persons converted to Judaism. It was for them a ritual of purification, but also a means of signifying a new birth, drowning to the person they had been and coming out of the water "born anew" as a Jew. *Mikva'ot* are still found within strands of Judaism today and are used for the reasons described above.

As time went on, this type of washing took on new meanings, and its symbolism expanded. John adapted Moses' ritual of bathing and broadened its meaning and application. For his followers it was an expression of their desire to repent, yet also a sign of God's forgiveness and grace. Early Christians continued to add new layers of meaning and to reinterpret this act for the next few centuries after the time of Christ.

Standing at the Jordan River, in the place where John baptized, it struck me that there was undoubtedly a host of additional interpretations and symbolic meanings of baptism that occurred to people as they came to the river. Allow me briefly to recount a few of the ideas going through my head as I stood in the Jordan, thinking about people who had come to be baptized by John.

When you stand in the Jordan, you can see the water flowing south, and in just a couple of miles it empties into the Dead Sea, where the high mineral content ensures that virtually nothing survives. The imagery is powerful: your sins are being washed away to the Dead Sea, along with your guilt, never to be held against you again and ideally no longer having power over you. Surely some early Christians were thinking this as they stood by, waiting to wade into the water.

It was at or near this spot on the Jordan that the Israelites crossed from the wilderness to the Promised Land, leaving behind their former lives as slaves and emerging as a free people, with a land to call their own. Surely there were some early Christians who, like the Israelites, sensed that they were no longer slaves but free.

And for those whose friends had been baptized upon conversion to Judaism, at least some might have seen in this baptism a new birth and a chance to begin anew. Jesus, having experienced this baptism himself, spoke of the importance of being spiritually reborn—born of water and the Spirit.

Perhaps it was the imagery of death and resurrection that some saw. Paul certainly saw this years later as he reflected upon the meaning of Christian baptism. Paul observed that in baptism we die to the person we have been. We identify with Jesus' death. We are buried with him. And, as we come out of the water, we are raised up with him. Maybe those being baptized by John felt this sense of death and resurrection.

There is a wealth of images and theological ideas that appear in the Bible related to the use of water as a means of ritual cleansing, an expression of repentance and forgiveness, and a rite of initiation into the Christian faith.

John stood by the Jordan River, playing the part of the promised Elijah, announcing God's kingdom and inviting people to repent and return to God's path. He called them to "revere God's name" so that the "sun of righteousness" would rise "with healing in its wings," and the people, once healed, would leap "like calves from the stall" (Malachi 4:2 NRSV).

His was a voice crying in the wilderness, "Prepare the way of the Lord" and declaring that "one who is more powerful than I is coming after me; I am not worthy to carry his sandals" (Mark 1:3 NRSV; Matthew 3:11 NRSV).

John's Message

John's preaching, empowered by the Spirit, deeply affected those who came to hear him. The message was the same that Jesus would soon be preaching: "Repent, for the kingdom of heaven has come near." John's message was urgent. Because God's reign—his kingdom and soon his Prince—was about to break onto the scene, people must repent. They must turn away from sin and turn toward God.

The Greek word for repentance is *metanoia*—literally, to think differently or to change one's mind. But it means something deeper than this in the Gospels. It means to have a change of mind that leads to a change of heart and a change of values that ultimately leads to a changed life.

Why did John call the people to repent, and what led them to respond? Perhaps here it is helpful to recall that the word for sin in the Greek New Testament is *hamartia*. It means to miss the mark or to stray from a path. In English, the word *sin* carries a lot of baggage—meanings that may or may not have been intended in the Bible. But in Greek the meaning is much simpler, and virtually all of us, religious or not, can see how it relates to our lives. Implied in the idea of straying from the path or missing the mark is that there *is* a path or mark—an ideal that we are meant to live by. I haven't met anyone who disagrees with this concept. All honest and thoughtful people will recognize that at times they stray from this path. In fact, the biblical story is largely about humanity's straying from the path, beginning when Adam and Eve ate the forbidden fruit, and God's call for the human race to get back on the path—to repent.

Those who heard John and were moved by his call to repent asked him, "What must we do?" In other words, if we've been off course, what does the right course look like? Luke 3 preserves for us the words of John as he responded to their questions. His words help us to grasp John's understanding of the path of righteousness. He said to the crowds, "The man with two tunics should share with him who has none, and the one who has food should do the same" (Luke 3:11 NIV). The fruit God was looking for—the evidence that one was seeking to live for God—was found in being generous toward the poor and demonstrating a concern for them.

There were tax collectors who came to John to be baptized. This was a remarkable thing and a prelude to the ministry of Jesus, who befriended them. Publicans or tax collectors were considered traitors to their people and were notorious for their heavy-handed tactics, for their love of money, and for their willingness to demand more than was due. Yet there were many of them who felt spiritually hungry and longed to be right with God. They came to the river and asked John, "What must we do?" And John told them not to collect more than was due.

Soldiers, too, came to John. Were these Roman soldiers, or perhaps those who worked for the religious leaders or Herod Antipas? We don't know. What we do know is that, like the tax collectors, these men were spiritually hungry, were moved by the call to repent and return to God's path, and were prepared to wade into the waters of the Jordan as an expression of their desire to walk in God's way. They too asked, "What must we do?" John's response: "Do not extort money from anyone by threats or false accusation, and be satisfied with your wages" (Luke 3:14 NRSV).

What is interesting in all three of these responses is that the path to which John called each group (and hence the path they had strayed from, prior to repentance) had something to do with money and material possessions. The common people were not helping those in need. The tax collectors were taking more in taxes than was due, in order to enrich themselves. And the soldiers were using their power to extort money from the people. Greed, in other words, was the common theme in John's preaching. Matthew adds religious hypocrisy to Luke's list of the people's sins, but that charge was leveled at the religious leaders who had come to observe John's preaching and unorthodox baptisms.

John's words are timeless. Our world, including the church, continues to miss the mark. We still need John's call to repent. This is why his story is often told during the season of Advent, as Christians prepare to celebrate Christmas—because Advent is a time of preparing one's heart for the birth of Jesus. His story is also told during Lent, when Christians smudge their foreheads with ashes as a sign of both their repentance and mortality. In so doing, we symbolically join all who came to hear John preach and repented when they heard him. Lent is a chance to acknowledge that we have strayed from the path and want to return to the path once more.

What is the path we have strayed from? John the Baptist told us, as did the prophet Isaiah before him: "Prepare the way for the Lord; make his paths straight" (Luke 3:4 CEB). Jesus himself told us: "I am the way, the truth, and the life" (John 14:6 CEB).

The way.

It's what John pointed toward. It's what is meant by the title of this book. It's what Jesus showed us as he walked the hills, valleys, and mountains of Palestine–teaching, preaching, healing, showing us the face of God.

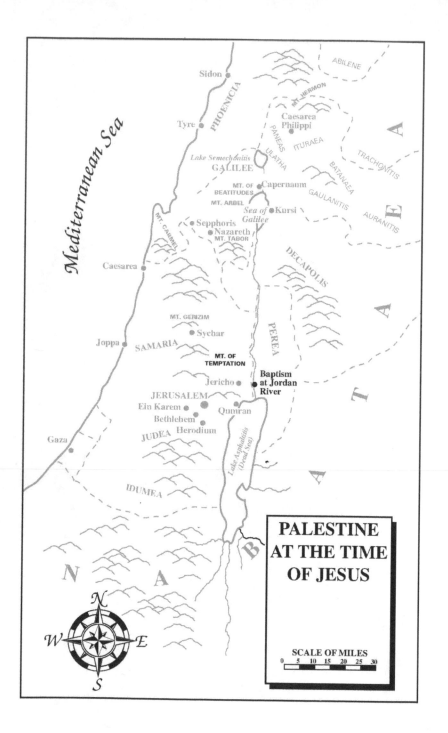

Mediterranean Sea

Sidon

PHOENICIA

ABILENE

MT. HERMON

Tyre

Caesarea
Philippi

PANEAS

ITURAEA

ULATHA

TRACHONITIS

Lake Semechonitis

GALILEE

BATANAEA

MT. OF
BEATITUDES

Capernaum

GAULANITIS

AURANITIS

MT. ARBEL

Sea of
Galilee

Kursi

Sepphoris

Nazareth

MT. TABOR

DECAPOLIS

MT. CARMEL

Caesarea

MT. GERIZIM

Sychar

PEREA

Joppa

SAMARIA

MT. OF
TEMPTATION

Jericho

Baptism
at Jordan
River

JERUSALEM

Ein Karem

Qumran

Bethlehem

Herodium

Gaza

JUDEA

Lake Asphaltitis
(Dead Sea)

IDUMEA

N

A

B

A

N

W

E

S

PALESTINE
AT THE TIME
OF JESUS

SCALE OF MILES

0   5   10 15 20 25 30

1. Baptism and Temptation
The Jordan River and the Wilderness

In those days Jesus came from <u>Nazareth</u> in Galilee and was <u>baptized</u> by <u>John</u> in the <u>Jordan</u>. And just as he was coming up out of the water, he saw the <u>heavens</u> <u>torn</u> <u>apart</u> and the <u>Spirit</u> descending like a dove on him. And a voice came from heaven, "<u>You are my Son, the Beloved; with you I am well pleased</u>." And the Spirit immediately drove him out into the <u>wilderness</u>, and he was in the <u>wilderness forty days</u>, being tempted by Satan.

Mark 1:9-13 NRSV

ONE DAY, AS JOHN WAS BAPTIZING in the Jordan, he looked up to see a familiar face. He smiled as Jesus approached, and the two men embraced. These men had known one another their entire lives. They had played together as boys and dreamed together as young men. John was six months older, but he always knew it was his younger cousin who would play the greater role in God's plans. The two had shared long walks and conversations both in Jerusalem and in the monastery by the Salt Sea. They had stayed up long into the night discussing the Scriptures and the kingdom of God. John's preaching and baptism at the Jordan would officially set in motion a chain of events that would lead to John's own death in a matter of months, and to Jesus' crucifixion just three years later.

Jesus took off his sandals and robe and said to John, "Baptize me, brother!" John stepped back, confused, protesting: "I need to be baptized by you, and do you come to me?" Jesus insisted, "Let it be so now; for it is proper for us in this way to fulfill all righteousness" (Matthew 3:14, 15 NRSV). With his baptism, the three-year public ministry of Jesus began. From this time on, the die was cast. The prospect was exciting, and terrifying. Jesus was thirty years of age when he waded into the waters of the Jordan to be baptized by his older cousin.

Even in the first century, Christians were unsettled by John's baptism of Jesus. They wondered, as modern-day disciples do, why one who "knew no sin" received a baptism, indicating a repentance of sin.

In Jesus' baptism, the sinless man chose to identify with sinful people. He stepped into the water not out off his need but for ours. Later he would tell his disciples that "the Son of Man came to seek and to save the lost" (Luke 19:10 NIV). He wasn't embarrassed to identify with sinners by wading into the waters of repentance. He didn't announce to every-

28

one present, "I don't really need this; it's for you." He chose to let others think what they would—he was walking into the water with us and for us. In the days ahead, he would eat with sinners and tax collectors. He would befriend prostitutes and adulterers. This was his mission. In his baptism, Jesus identified with sinners.

At the church that I serve, we have support groups for people with various addictions. If you had friends who struggled with sexual addiction, and you knew they might find help and deliverance by attending a support group, would you offer to go with them to the group? Would you worry what others might think as they saw you enter the room? Would you feel the need to say, "I'm with them. I don't really have a sexual addiction. I'm just their friend"? Or would you sit quietly with your friends, hoping and praying that because you were there with them, they might find help? In essence, this is what Jesus did when he was baptized. He identified with sinners, not only joining them in the water, but also inviting all who would follow him to wade in.

Baptism has many meanings. Like a kaleidoscope, it presents a different picture with each turn. As Jesus stepped into the water to identify with sinful humanity and become the Son of Man, the Holy Spirit descended upon him like a dove. He heard the voice of God announcing that he was God's beloved son, with whom God was "well pleased" (Luke 3:22). Thus, in that moment Jesus was declaring that he was the Son of Man while God was declaring that he was the Son of God. Jesus also received power from the Spirit for the ministry that lay ahead. Here at the Jordan, we see the first glimpse of what Christians would come to call the Trinity. The Son came to be baptized. The Father spoke. The Spirit descended.

The Jordan River

Most Christians who visit the Holy Land have gone to the Jordan River to remember the baptism of Jesus and their own baptism. Until recently nearly all these pilgrims visited a site just south of the Sea of Galilee called Yardenit. It is a beautiful place, with trees and with water that is relatively clear and perhaps one hundred feet across. Robes, changing rooms, towels, and showers make this a great place to step into the Jordan. But this is not where John baptized Jesus (or anyone else). If you want to experience the Jordan as it was when Jesus was baptized, in the place at or near where he was baptized, you'll need to travel sixty-five miles south of there, to a newly opened site on the Jordan near Jericho.

Here the river is about twenty feet wide and no more than four to five feet deep (except in the spring). It has thickets of reeds on either side, and the water runs the color of a cup of green tea with cream.

On the Jordanian side of the river, the ruins of Byzantine churches have been found pointing toward this as an ancient site where Christians came to remember their baptisms. New churches have been constructed there. The Israeli bank was covered in mines for the last forty years, but now these have been removed and a modest pavilion has been set up for Christians to recall the baptism of Jesus. A small gift shop sells robes and towels. Cold showers are outside to rinse off after stepping in the Jordan. Jordanian soldiers stand watch on one side of the river, Israeli on the other, as Christians from around the world come, one bus at a time, to remember the baptism of Christ.

In the DVD that is available to accompany this book, I take you to this site. When I visited it was February, and I had the site to myself. The temperature that day was in the sixties, and so was the water temperature. As I stepped into the water, the feel of the riverbed struck me as my feet sank into the soft, smooth soil. I suspect it felt much the same to Jesus, John, and the thousands John baptized. I immersed myself in the water to remember my own baptism and to identify with Jesus, who was baptized by John in this place.

Beloved of God

The words spoken by God at Jesus' baptism come, at least in part, from Psalm 2:7, a coronation song in which the psalmist speaks of the kings of Israel as God's sons. But it is not an exact quote. The Psalm says, "You are my Son; today I have become your Father" (Psalm 2:7 NRSV). But to Jesus, God spoke in the midst of his baptism, saying "You are my Son, *the Beloved,* with you I am *well pleased*" (Mark 1:11 NRSV, emphasis added).

Jesus was "beloved" of God. The word used was *agapetos*—a Greek adjective that is a term of endearment signifying a special and deep bond with a favorite person, one who is treasured and dear. God reaffirmed this special relationship with Jesus at the Mount of Transfiguration, not long before Jesus' death, by using the Greek verb *eudokeo.* The word indicates taking particular delight or pleasure in someone or something.

Recently our oldest daughter Danielle and her husband moved back to Kansas City after being away for several years. They returned to the area so Danielle could go to graduate school. Having her back has brought great joy to my wife LaVon and me. I gave Danielle a big hug the other day and told her, "I love you so much. I feel such joy that you are back in Kansas City and I get to see you regularly." To me, this is the sense that *agapetos* and *eudokeo* carry with them; this is what Jesus was hearing from God.

For Jesus, his baptism was a defining act. In that moment, he identified with sinners and heard God's affirmation that he was the Father's beloved son. He received the Spirit's power. And it marked the beginning of his ministry. Jesus' baptism was an ordination in which he was set aside and empowered for his mission of drawing people to God, inviting them into God's kingdom, demonstrating God's will, and ultimately laying down his life for humanity.

For us, as Christ followers, baptism is also meant as a defining act. Through our baptism we are claimed by God, anointed with the Spirit, and set aside for God's purposes. Our brokenness is recognized and God's grace is promised. And in our baptisms we are initiated into, and become a part of, God's covenant people. We are meant to remember our baptisms each day. Even if we don't remember the act of baptism itself, we remember that God has promised to forgive our sins, that we are called to ministry, that the Holy Spirit resides in us, and that we are God's children.

It is said that Martin Luther, when he struggled with bouts of depression, would look into the mirror when he was at his lowest and say to himself, "Martin Luther, you are baptized. Don't forget it." Several years ago, when preaching on baptism, I invited our members to remember their baptism each day. To help them do so, we prepared a simple prayer and printed it on a plastic card with a rubber band attached. We invited our members to hang this prayer in their shower and to recite the prayer when they stepped into the water each morning. The card says,

✝ Lord, as I enter the water to bathe, I remember my baptism.

Wash me by your grace. Fill me with your Spirit. Renew my soul.

I pray that I might live as your child today and honor you in all that I do.

We give these shower tag prayers to our graduating high school seniors each year so that, when they go off to college, each morning as they take a shower they will remember their baptisms and, in so doing, remember who they are. They are children of God and a part of the family of Christ.

Led to the Wilderness

The Scripture tells us that Jesus, immediately following what must have been one of the most spiritually significant experiences of his life, was led (or driven) by the Spirit to the wilderness to be tempted while fasting for forty days and forty nights. Many of you will be reading this book during the season of Lent. The Christian season of Lent is a forty-day period, excluding Sundays, in which Christ followers join Jesus on his forty-day fast, spiritually walking in his footsteps. Lent is a season of repentance and spiritual self-examination. It is a time to draw near to Christ, and a time when we recall our brokenness and mortality. This allows us to appreciate the blessings that come on Good Friday and Easter, when Christ dies for us and then is raised to life.

As we retrace Jesus' footsteps during his forty days in the wilderness, we'll learn something about where he spent the forty days and why he went there, and we'll consider the nature and meaning of his wrestling match with the devil.

Jesus left John at the Jordan River and hiked five miles due west across a flat desert dotted with scrub brush. The desert likely looks the same today as it did when Jesus began his journey. In this area one might pass a camel or two, or a shepherd grazing his sheep, but otherwise there's not a lot to see between the Jordan River and the mountains of the wilderness. According to tradition Jesus would have passed on the north side of Jericho, the desert oasis town. He would also have come very close to the Wadi Qelt, where King Herod had built a fabulous winter palace, a palace that was at that time still in use by his family, the ruins of which you can visit to this day.

Just north of Jericho, the first of many Judean wilderness mountains arises. It is a rugged and barren mountain, known today as Mount Qurantal. (*Qurantal* means forty; the mountain is so named because it is thought that Jesus spent his forty days of temptation here.) It is often referred to simply as the Mount of Temptation.

Some people who read that Jesus spent forty days and nights in the wilderness picture an overgrown tropical forest. But the wilderness of Judea is a desert, dry and arid, that looks something like the Badlands of South Dakota or one of many places in the desert southwest of the United States. This is where Jesus would spend the next forty days and forty nights fasting, praying, and wrestling with the devil.

Halfway up Mount Qurantal is a large cave, easily seen from the base of the mountain. The tradition going back at least to the 300s is that Jesus slept there during his forty days. Certainly this was the closest large cave in the wilderness to the place where Jesus was baptized.

Today the Monastery of the Temptation clings to the side of the mountain and covers the cave. Pilgrims can walk up, as Jesus did, or ride a tram. I took that walk with a group of pilgrims on a recent trip. Once inside the monastery, we went past rooms belonging to Orthodox monks until coming to the entrance of the large cave. Partway back into the cave, which is set up as a chapel, is an iron gate. It is opened at various times during the day for service or for visitors to go deeper into the cave. At the back of this large cave is an opening and several stairs down. All but children have to duck their heads as they enter. Here is a smaller cave, which I judged to be about three feet by six feet with a height of about five feet. This smaller cave is said to be where Jesus slept during his forty days and forty nights in the wilderness.

I was fortunate to have the space to myself for a few moments, and I tried to imagine Christ sleeping here. Scattered throughout the room were photos brought by visitors of loved ones they were praying for and scraps of paper bearing prayer requests. I paused for a moment there to pray and to thank Christ for choosing to undergo the temptations, and I invited him to strengthen me when I face the tempter.

As I left the Monastery of the Temptation, I walked down a path where most visitors don't go. It took me back to the mountainside, just below the monastery. I imagined Jesus walking this desolate path, with nothing to eat or drink, sleeping alone in a cave, and I was reminded that the wilderness is often a metaphor for those places we don't want to go, when life seems barren and the road seems hard and we seem to be wrestling with evil.

I thought of Elijah, who fled to the wilderness when the evil Queen Jezebel sought to kill him. I remembered David, who fled from Saul and lived among the caves, writing psalms with words such as "How long, O Lord? Will you forget me forever?" I thought about Moses, living for those long years as a fugitive from Pharoah's hand in the wilderness of Sinai. All these stories have one thing in common: God met each of these men as they sojourned in the wilderness. What was true for them is true for us. All of us sojourn in the wilderness at times in our lives, feeling hopeless and all alone. Yet when we pay attention and listen, God comes to us and uses the wilderness to strengthen and sanctify us.

The Judean Wilderness

Did Jesus stay in the cave for forty days and forty nights? There is so much rugged beauty all around the Judean wilderness that I suspect if he stayed there, it was only for a few days. There are places far more enticing and impressive as you walk a few hours farther into the wilderness. But the cave gives us an anchor, a placeholder to remember that Jesus came to the wilderness, somewhere around this place, to walk and pray and be tempted.

As I was in the Holy Land retracing Jesus' footsteps for this book, I spent hours in the wilderness visiting places I had never seen before. It was one of the most beautiful places I've ever been—absolutely captivating. I felt a connection with Moses, who spent nearly all his adult life in the wilderness of the Sinai, and with David, who composed many of his psalms in the Judean wilderness. I could see how Elijah would hear the "still small voice" of God in this place, and why John the Baptist chose to live his life here.

Beginning in the late third century, spiritually hungry Christ followers began to live in caves in the deserts of Egypt, Palestine, and Syria. These followers were called the Desert Fathers. At one time several thousand lived in the wilderness of Judea, identifying with John and Jesus as they devoted themselves to prayer and the pursuit of God.

If you visit the Holy Land, ask your guide if it would be possible, while in Jerusalem or Jericho, to visit the wilderness above the monastery of St. George along the Wadi Qelt, and plan to spend time there walking and praying in silence, remembering John's life in the wilderness and Jesus' forty days being tempted. The wilderness is not far off the road linking Jerusalem to Jericho, and it is well worth the trip.

The Meaning of the Three Temptations

Jesus spent forty days in the wilderness. The number is significant. The rain that raised Noah's ark fell for forty days and forty nights. Moses spent forty days and forty nights fasting on Mount Sinai as he received the Law. Elijah fasted for forty days and forty nights in the wilderness before hearing God whisper to him. In addition to these examples, there was one more connection to the number forty that may have been important. The children of Israel wandered in the wilderness for forty years. In Deuteronomy 8:2, Moses says that that period of wandering was to test them, "to know what was in your heart, whether or not you would keep his commandments" (NRSV). This last connection seems to have been foremost in Jesus' mind, for in his responses to the devil's temptations we find that all three of his responses came from Deuteronomy, chapters 6 to 8.

Jesus' temptations and his time in the wilderness were a way for him to connect with the stories of the holy people of old, but they meant more than that. The temptations served as a test for Jesus. Just as a teacher gives a test, not to break students but to strengthen them, so it was with this test. (The Greek word for temptation, *peirazo*, is often translated as "testing.") Jesus was being tempted, but more important he was being tested, so that when he began his public ministry and faced adversity and success, he would continue steadfast in his mission.

When you think of Jesus' temptations, how do you imagine them? The Gospels describe a conversation between Jesus and the devil. We might take this literally and at face value. But it seems more likely that Jesus had a conversation with the devil in the same way we have conversations with the devil. I don't see a man in red tights, carrying a pitchfork. I hear a whisper to do something I have no business doing or urging me to refrain from doing what I should do. He personifies the inner spiritual struggles that all of us face. We've all wrestled with the devil.

We don't know all the temptations the devil threw at Jesus over those forty days, but Matthew and Luke tell us of three specific temptations. Unless they were simply making it up, the only way they could have known this information was for Jesus to have described his wrestling match with the devil to his disciples. I think this is likely. And if he did so, he was trying to teach them something about temptation, and he was also revealing something about his own temptations, which can be seen as the archetypal or universal struggles we wrestle with as human beings.

Jesus' first temptation was about food. Food is among our most basic needs, but the desire for it can at times be our undoing. This first temptation takes us back to the Garden of Eden, where Adam and Eve were tested by the tempter, who urged them to eat the forbidden fruit. They succumbed to the temptation, ate the fruit, and paradise was lost. Several chapters later in Genesis, Esau was willing to sell his birthright to his brother Jacob for a bowl of porridge. In Exodus, the Israelites were willing to return to slavery in Egypt so they could eat cucumbers and leeks rather than manna. In each of these stories, the desire for instant gratification that was related to food led to (or in the case of the Israelites in the wilderness, would have led to) a profound loss of blessing.

Those of us who live in the developed world struggle with the temptations related to food. We are tempted to eat too much, or to eat the kinds of food that increase the likelihood of disease. We know this but find it hard to say no to the devil's whispers. Meanwhile our eating habits have helped cause a health-care crisis. We also know that millions of people die of starvation and malnutrition each year, yet few of us give to causes that benefit those in extreme poverty.

Jesus was hungry after fasting for forty days. He was tempted to break his fast and use his power to feed himself. He knew what it was to be tempted by food. Yet he resisted, which later made it possible for Jesus to tell his disciples, "Do not worry about your life, what you will eat or what you will drink, or about your body, what you will wear. Is not life more than food, and the body more than clothing?" Jesus' response to the devil when tempted by food was to quote from Moses' words in Deuteronomy 8:3: "One does not live by bread alone, but by every word that comes from the mouth of the Lord" (NRSV).

In the second temptation, the devil invited Jesus to jump off the pinnacle of the Temple. This temptation can be understood in one of two ways. It may represent the nearly universal tendency to win affirmation and affection by doing dangerous stunts. When I was growing up, once or twice a year a showman named Evel Knievel would get on his motorcycle and jump across a football field, and later across a river and a canyon. The whole nation would watch this guy, who broke over four hundred bones during the course of his life. Today, millions tune in to television shows broadcasting the exploits of people who are willing to eat the most disgusting things and do the most dangerous things, in order to win a prize and claim their fifteen minutes of fame. I'm not knocking this. I'm suggesting that it's one way to win friends and influence people, and that jumping off the pinnacle of the Temple may have been the archetype of the reality show. However, God was calling Jesus to "win friends and influence people" not by a foolish stunt, but by bearing a crown of thorns in an act of sacrificial love.

Jesus' second temptation may also be understood in a different way. Have you ever stood on a high building and had the urge, just for a moment, to jump? As terrifying as that urge may be, there seems to be in each of us an odd and morbid temptation to test fate—or, for some, a more serious temptation to end it all. I wonder if Jesus, at a very subtle level, might have been tempted to jump, knowing that either God would deliver him, or his life would be over without having to endure the journey that lay ahead. If this were the case, then the archetypal temptation here is suicide. At the very least, Jesus stood on the ledge of the building and thought for a moment about jumping. When I minister with people who are suicidal, it has struck me that this may be a helpful insight into the temptation they are fighting—that Jesus knew what it was to stand on the ledge and seriously to consider jumping. But Jesus, choosing instead to see the difficult journey ahead through the eyes of faith and realizing that God would redeem his suffering, did not jump.

Finally we have the last of the temptations recorded in the Gospels, though we can be sure that Jesus knew many other temptations in his life and ministry. This last is the archetypal temptation to sell one's soul for wealth and power. Listen to this temptation as told by Matthew: "The devil took him to a very high mountain and showed him all the kingdoms of the world and their splendor; and he said to him, 'All these I will give you, if you will fall down and worship me'" (4:8-9 NRSV).

This final temptation is like the first temptation for food and drink, but it goes far beyond that. This is the temptation that drives so many in our world today. Many who start life with the best of intentions find the allure of wealth and power to be irresistible. Jesus was told that if he would only bow down and worship the devil, he could have it all. And undoubtedly he could have. Imagine if Jesus had yielded to this temptation, using his gifts for his own gain and basing his life on an abundance of possessions. He would have been fabulously wealthy and gained immense power, and the world would have continued its relentless march toward self-destruction.

Whether we spend our tithes and offerings on lottery tickets, or we cheat on our taxes, or we misrepresent our products and services, or we pretend to be something we're not in order to further our quest for financial gain, most of us have struggled with this temptation.

Jesus responded to the devil with these words: "Away with you, Satan! For it is written, 'Worship the Lord your God, and serve only him'" (Matthew 4:10 NRSV). Jesus was angry. Perhaps he was irritated with the tempter's games, or maybe this was the most appealing and threatening of the temptations. I suspect the latter because of the number of times Jesus addressed this topic in the Gospels. Often, my most powerful sermons are addressed to me first. Jesus did not need to preach to himself, but he did know the lure of wealth and power, and that lure undoubtedly shaped his teaching that one "cannot serve God and mammon" (Matthew 6:24 NKJV).

We all have moments when we wrestle with the devil. During those moments, God speaks to us through Scripture, through other people, and through the "still small voice." Yet the devil, as we've seen in the temptation story, speaks to us in those same ways: through Scripture (the devil, as he did with Jesus, is a master at proof-texting, taking minor points of Scripture and using them to override more important texts), through other people, and through his own whispers in our head.

Jesus countered these tempting thoughts and rebuked the tempter by quoting Scripture. (Interestingly, all the Scriptures that Jesus used with the devil came from Deuteronomy 6–8, in which Moses stood just across the Jordan River from the place where Jesus was being tempted.) I find that Scripture is a pretty good place to start in my own struggles with the tempter.

Jesus' temptations in the wilderness were meant to test his resolve, not with the aim of weakening him, but in order to strengthen him. When we fast and pray and stare down our own temptations, we find it does the same for us.

It's comforting to know that Jesus felt the power of these temptations. As the writer of Hebrews says in 4:15-16: "We do not have a high priest who is unable to sympathize with our weaknesses, but we have one who in every respect has been tested as we are, yet without sin. Let us therefore approach the throne of grace with boldness, so that we may receive mercy and find grace to help in time of need" (NRSV).

Walking in the footsteps of Jesus begins with baptism but will inevitably include temptation. The way of Christ includes striving to resist temptation. Yet when we do succumb to temptation, we "approach the throne of grace with boldness, so that we may receive mercy" from the one who knew temptation.

Reflection
Baptism and Forgiveness

> John the baptizer appeared in the wilderness, proclaiming a
> baptism of repentance for the forgiveness of sins. And people
> from the whole Judean countryside and all the people of
> Jerusalem were going out to him, and were baptized by him
> in the river Jordan, confessing their sins. (Mark 1:4-5 NRSV)

The Jordan River, where John was baptizing, was an
eight-hour walk through the desert from Jerusalem. Yet
Mark tells us that many from Jerusalem made the trek
to hear John preach and to be immersed by him in the
Jordan. Why did they walk eight hours, some more, to
answer John's call to repent?

John dressed in the garments of a prophet. He spoke
powerfully. People came believing that God had sent this
man, and that his message was from God. He called the
people to repent and to be baptized for the forgiveness of
their sins. What John offered at the Jordan was God's forgiveness and a chance to begin anew. Which of us doesn't
long for this at times?

She was in her thirties and had lived a hard life. She
began attending our church, yearning for a new beginning.

She had come to be baptized, and I spoke with her about the meaning of this act. In my tribe (Methodists), baptism has a kaleidoscope of meanings. Among these, it is a dramatic sign of God's grace and mercy—his willingness to wash us and make us new. It is an outward sign of God's forgiveness.

As she approached the baptistery she had tears in her eyes. She asked, "Pastor Adam, does God really forgive all that I've done? I've done a lot of terrible things." I assured her that as she came to God, repentant, he would forgive it all. And I reminded her that Christian baptism is a sign not only of God's forgiveness for sins in the past, but a promise of forgiveness when, in the future, we stumble and need his grace. And thus, with her baptism, she began a new life.

Do you ever feel a yearning for forgiveness and a new beginning? Every morning as I step into the shower, I remember my baptism and ask God to wash me and make me new. At times I feel a profound sense of my own sin and my longing for his grace. At other times I simply know that there are ways in which I have not lived up to his calling on my life. Either way, I recall with gratitude God's forgiveness and his claim upon my life.

If you have yet to be baptized, speak with your pastor about this profound act. If you have been baptized, remember your baptism each day as you bathe, inviting God, once again, to wash you and cover you by his grace.

Lord, in thought, word, and deed, by what I have done and what I have left undone, I have sinned against you and others. Remember the promise you made at my baptism, and wash me anew. I call upon the grace you offer us in Jesus Christ. Amen.

From *The Way: 40 Days of Reflection*. Abingdon Press, 2012.

Travel Photos

Qumran, where John the Baptist may have lived with the Essenes

Mikveh, a baptistry used in Essene rites of purification

Jordan River location where Jesus may have been baptized

Judean Wilderness

Monastery of the Temptation, on Mount Qurantal, the Mount of Temptation

Inner cave at Mount Qurantal, where tradition says Jesus slept

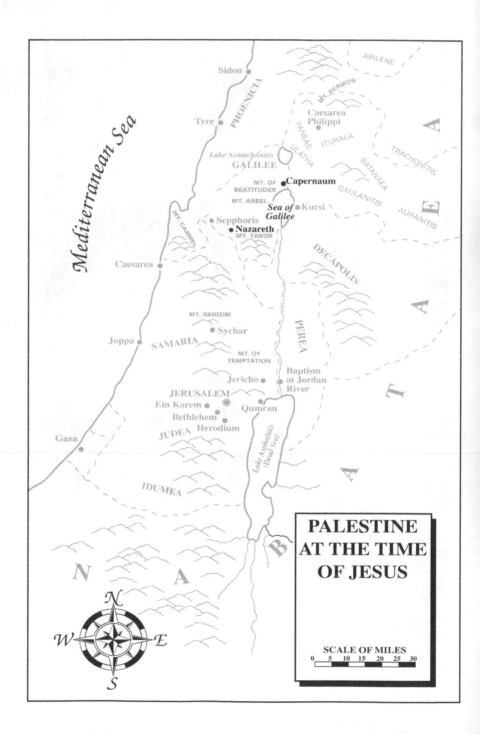

PALESTINE AT THE TIME OF JESUS

2. The Healing Ministry
Capernaum

Now when Jesus heard that John had been arrested, he withdrew to Galilee. He left Nazareth and made his home in Capernaum by the sea.

Matthew 4:12-13 NRSV

They went to Capernaum; and when the sabbath came, he entered the synagogue and taught. They were astounded at his teaching, for he taught them as one having authority, and not as the scribes. Just then there was in their synagogue a man with an unclean spirit, and he cried out, "What have you to do with us, Jesus of Nazareth? Have you come to destroy us? I know who you are, the Holy One of God." But Jesus rebuked him, saying, "Be silent, and come out of him!"

Mark 1:21-25 NRSV

As soon as they left the synagogue, they entered the house of Simon and Andrew, with James and John. Now Simon's mother-in-law was in bed with a fever, and they told him about her at once. He came and took her by the hand and lifted her up. Then the fever left her, and she began to serve them. That evening, at sunset, they brought to him all who were sick or possessed with demons.

Mark 1:29-32 NRSV

SHORTLY AFTER JESUS' FORTY days of temptation, John the Baptist was arrested, and Jesus decided to return to his hometown of Nazareth, in the region of Galilee. Nazareth was a small, working-class village of perhaps one hundred to two hundred people, many of whom were related. It was considered "the other side of the tracks" relative to Sephoris, a nearby town of 30,000 that was known as the Jewel of the Galilee.

Nazareth was so insignificant that it wasn't included in lists of towns of the Galilee. In John's Gospel, when Nathaniel was told by Philip that Jesus of Nazareth was the Messiah, Nathaniel replied, "Can anything good come out of Nazareth?" (John 1:46 NRSV). It was to this insignificant town that Jesus returned, filled with the Spirit, ready to call people to repentance and usher in the kingdom of God.

That Sabbath the small synagogue in Nazareth was crowded with people who had come to hear Jesus preach. Luke tells us he opened the Isaiah scroll to the place where the prophet had written:

The Spirit of the Lord is upon me,
because he has anointed me
to bring good news to the poor.

He has sent me to proclaim release to the captives
  and recovery of sight to the blind,
  to let the oppressed go free,
  to proclaim the year of the Lord's favor.
                                    (Luke 4:18-19 NRSV)

Jesus read these words and then paused, as everyone waited to hear his message. He stunned them by saying simply, "Today this scripture has been fulfilled in your hearing" (Luke 4:21 NRSV).

Jesus, in no uncertain terms, claimed that he was the long-awaited Messiah. Can you imagine how those words sounded to the people who had watched him grow up? Some of the townspeople spoke well of him, but others wondered how he could claim such a thing. Some called it blasphemy. Hearing this, Jesus invoked a story about how Elijah, unable to find faithful people among the Israelites, took his ministry to a Gentile. In the same way, he said, "No prophet is accepted in his home town" (Luke 4:24 NIV). His words led some of the townspeople to seize him, take him to the edge of town, and threaten to throw him off a cliff!

I recall my first sermon in the little church where I came to faith. It's not easy preaching to people who saw you grow up. It's hard not to sound a bit "too big for your britches." Mine was truly a horrible sermon, but at least no one threatened to kill me. Jesus spoke with power and truth, and his cousins and neighbors and the folks who did business with his father wanted to kill him. He left Nazareth that day rejected by his own people. This is how Jesus' ministry began. It was a foreshadowing of things to come.

Matthew and Mark tell the story a bit differently from Luke. They record Jesus going to preach in his hometown after he'd been preaching and teaching around the Galilee, but the result was the same. When Jesus ministered in Nazareth, his own people turned him away.

A Lonely Journey

Jesus left his hometown that day, rejected and alone. He made his way along the Sea of Galilee, toward a town on the northwest shore called *Kfar Nahum*—Capernaum.

As Jesus drew near to the Sea of Galilee he would have taken the road that wound through the Valley of the Doves, with Mount Arbel to the right and Mount Nitai to the left. The valley is beautiful, with a stream running through it. In some ways the valley is like the wilderness of Judea, but its lush trees and flowering plants make it a place that beckons you to pray. On either side of the valley, midway up the mountains, are sheer cliffs with caves where rebels against King Herod had hidden not long before the birth of Jesus and where, two hundred years after the Master walked there, monks would take up residence. If Jesus walked near these caves on Mount Arbel, he would have seen the entire northern half of the Sea of Galilee; in fact, aside from the events of Jesus' final week, 80 percent of the Gospel stories would take place in the towns he could see from that vantage point. (This is a fact I always find amazing: that everything we read in the Gospels occurred in a geographic area no larger than the greater Kansas City metropolitan area where I live, and most of his ministry was in what we would consider very small towns.)

The Valley of the Doves empties into a plain along the Sea of Galilee at the lakeshore village of Magdala. What did Jesus do when he arrived in Magdala? There were no disciples yet who could record the events. It is possible that Jesus stayed for the night before going on to Capernaum. Certainly he would have stopped for a meal and to rest. But I would suggest that while he was there, he also stopped to heal a woman.

The woman was afflicted with demons, seven of them. Whether these literally were spiritual entities or were a variety of mental and physical afflictions, she clearly was oppressed. Jesus, seeing the woman, stopped to speak with her. He cast out the pain, the voices, and the turmoil in her head and heart, and he healed her. The woman's name was Mary the Magdalene. In gratitude, Mary followed Jesus. She and several other women used their own means to support Jesus and the disciples as they traveled (Luke 8:2-3). Three years later, she stood by the cross as Jesus was crucified. Only John, among the disciples, had the courage to stand there with her. And it was this Mary who was the first witness to the Resurrection. I believe it was here, as Jesus came to Magdala with a heavy heart, having been rejected by his own, that he saw a woman, deranged, who likely had been rejected by her own, and he stopped to heal her.

Capernaum

Capernaum is the second-most important town in the Gospels (after Jerusalem but for very different reasons). Seven of the disciples were from there. Jesus called his first disciples while walking along the shorelines there. He taught in the synagogue there. He performed more miracles there—twelve of them—than anywhere else in the Gospels.

At that time Capernaum, or *Kfar Nahum* (Nahum's town) as it is called in Hebrew, was a town of 1,000 to 1,500 residents, with a harbor and 2,500 feet of seawall. Fishing was a mainstay, but the village was also known for its grain, its olives, and its craftsmen. The town, like several around the Sea of Galilee, was

Nazareth to Capernaum

Several years ago I decided to retrace the journey Jesus made after his rejection in Nazareth. The distance from Nazareth to Capernaum is about twenty-four miles. I started a bit to the north and east of Nazareth, in the town of Cana, where Jesus performed his first miracle by changing water into wine. I set out around noon, alone, carrying a backpack and a couple of bottles of water. Google Maps says the walk should take about eight hours, but I doubt that anyone from Google has ever tried it themselves! My total walking time was about twelve hours, divided over two days with a stay at a kibbutz hotel in between.

Today's highways in Israel and Palestine often follow the ancient roadways. Then, as now, roads were built along the easiest and shortest distance between two points. Most of the time my path was a half mile or so off the highway. As I walked that day, I kept thinking of what Jesus must have been feeling as he left Nazareth. I'd never considered the intense pain of that event, when the people Jesus had known his entire life rejected him, and some threatened to kill him. It must have been a lonely journey.

During that journey I was also struck by the vast amount of time Jesus spent walking during his ministry. The Gospels take just one sentence to tell us that Jesus went to Nazareth from the wilderness of Judea, but in fact it was a seven- or eight-day journey on foot. They tell us Jesus went from Nazareth to Capernaum: twelve hours. What did Jesus do during these long periods of walking? Before he called his disciples, I suspect he spent that time in prayer, often lost in thought about the Kingdom and his mission. After he called the disciples, as they walked together he would have been teaching and mentoring them.

As I walked from Magdala to Capernaum, I began by going along the sandy beach. But soon the lakeshore became covered with reeds, and so I joined a path away from the shore, following what is called the Jesus Trail. It led through groves of grapefruit, bananas, and oranges that were just north of the Sea of Galilee. At some point I lost the trail and wandered through open fields, where the remains of ancient villages could still be seen, awaiting exploration by archaeologists. Finally, beyond the fields, I arrived at the gates to the excavated ruins of Capernaum.

By the time I arrived at Capernaum I was exhausted and a bit dehydrated, having not packed enough water for the journey. I was hot, sweaty, and covered in dust. Yet I was also excited. I was standing in one of my favorite places in the Holy Land, the hometown of Jesus during his public ministry, as well as the location of so many of the Gospel stories.

The Franciscans are the caretakers of this archaeological site.[4] Their friars live there and hold mass daily in the contemporary church located in Capernaum. As I entered the ruins I spoke with a friar and asked him what it was like to live in the village where Jesus spent much of his public ministry. He became quite animated as he recounted the events that occurred in this town. He noted, "When walking among the ruins of Capernaum, you are literally walking where Jesus walked!"

largely constructed of black basalt that had been spewn from volcanoes when they erupted four million years ago. Based on the excavations to date, archaeologists believe the townspeople lived quite modestly, in houses averaging 500 to 600 square feet in size. We know from the Gospels that the town had a Roman customs office, and we even know the name of the customs officer in Jesus' day: Levi, who was also called Matthew, who became one of Jesus' disciples.

In another chapter we will consider Jesus' calling of his first disciples, but for now we'll simply remember that, according to Mark, as Jesus walked to Capernaum he saw Simon and Andrew standing on the seashore casting a net into the sea, and he invited them to come with him and become "fishers of people." The two men left their nets and followed Jesus. A bit closer to Capernaum he came across James and John, who sat in their fishing boat mending their nets. He called them, too, and they followed him.

For the next couple of days, Jesus may well have stayed at the home where Simon lived with his wife and her mother. We know nothing of what happened until the Sabbath, when Jesus was invited to the synagogue to teach.

Today, among the most impressive buildings in Capernaum are the ruins of a synagogue built around A.D. 300 of imported white limestone. It was constructed on top of, and apparently had dimensions similar to, the synagogue where Jesus ministered as recorded in the Gospels. Standing in the midst of the ruins, you are in the very place where Jesus taught and healed. I love to lead groups there and have them sit on benches that are built into the walls where the faithful sat centuries ago. It's a thrill to watch as the groups realize that they are sitting just above the place where stories from the Gospel occurred, such as the passage from Mark 1 at the beginning of this chapter.

Another fascinating site in modern Capernaum is just ninety feet from the synagogue. It is the ruins of an octagonal building from the Byzantine period, likely built in the 300s. Octagonal buildings from this time period are almost always churches. Christians in the Greco-Roman world considered seven to be the number of completeness—the seven days of the week and the seven orifices of the head (two eyes, two ears, two nostrils and one mouth) being examples of this completeness in creation. Eight was beyond completeness; it signified perfection. The Lord whom Christians served signified completeness and perfection as well. The eighth day of the week, which was also the first day of the week, Sunday, was the day of Christ's resurrection. The eight sides of this church and others like it would have reminded worshipers not only of God's perfection, but also of Christ's resurrection.

In 1968, excavations on this site beneath the level of the octagonal church revealed a first-century house. The house showed signs that it had been used as a place of worship before construction of the octagonal church. We know that during this period in the Holy Land, churches often were built on holy places from the life of Jesus. The question the archaeologists asked was this: What first-century house in Capernaum is mentioned or implied in the Gospels and would have been of such importance that Christians would built a church on top of it? The answer was the house where Jesus stayed while in Capernaum, which seems likely to have been the home of Simon Peter, his wife, and her mother, as well as Simon's brother, Andrew.[5] Pilgrims to this location in the late 300s noted a church built atop the house of St. Peter where the Lord had lived.

Clearly this is a remarkable archaeological site. Some years ago the Roman Catholic Church of St. Peter's House was built atop the site. The modern church, which looks a little bit like a spaceship, has a glass floor over the ruins, both to protect this important site and to help visitors recall that this place was Jesus' home during his public ministry. In viewing the ruins, visitors peer into, and symbolically join, the worship that took place in the church below. It is here that Christians believe the events of Mark 1:29-32 occurred:

> As soon as they left the synagogue, they entered the house of Simon and Andrew, with James and John. Now Simon's mother-in-law was in bed with a fever, and they told him about her at once. He came and took her by the hand and lifted her up. Then the fever left her, and she began to serve them. That evening, at sunset, they brought to him all who were sick or possessed with demons. (NRSV)

"Be Silent and Come Out of Him!"

Jesus was preaching and teaching in the synagogue at Capernaum. Women sat in the gallery above. Men sat on steps or benches built into the walls on three sides of the synagogue. Jesus would have stood to read Scripture and sat down to preach and teach. As he taught, Mark tells us, the people were astounded. The Greek word for "astounded," *thambeo,* is often used to describe the response of the people to Jesus. The English does not convey the entire meaning of the word, for it has a sense of instilling fear as well as wonder. When Jesus spoke, his words were powerful, disturbing, and authoritative.

Jesus' words were especially disturbing to one man who sat in their midst that Sabbath day. Mark tells us the man had an "unclean spirit," yet surprisingly he still had come to the synagogue to hear Jesus. In the middle of Jesus' message the man interrupted him, shouting, "What have you to do with us, Jesus of Nazareth? Have you come to destroy us? I know who you are, the Holy One of God!" (NRSV).

I have been interrupted on several occasions in the middle of a sermon—twice when people collapsed and others began shouting for help, and once when a man who was mentally ill walked to the front of the church as I was preaching, as though he had a question. In the first two cases we stopped the service to pray and seek medical help for the afflicted. In the case of the man, I stopped the sermon to ask if he needed anything. These experiences were a bit unnerving, but nothing compared to what happened in the synagogue that day!

Jesus spoke to the man, or to the personality or demon that spoke through him. In essence Jesus said, "Be silent, and come out of him!" The man convulsed and cried out, and whatever afflicted the man left him. The people watching were amazed (*thambeo*). They could not believe what they had just seen. Their response that day was far different from the response a week earlier in Nazareth. Jesus' fame spread quickly through the surrounding countryside, and soon huge crowds descended on Capernaum, searching for the teacher and healer from Nazareth.

This story, and others like it in the Gospels, raises questions for us in the twenty-first century. Jesus cast out demons as though they were a commonplace occurrence. Yet often the symptoms of demon possession look, to the modern eye, very much like symptoms from known physical or psychiatric disorders. Fevers were sometimes thought to be brought on by a demon. Being deaf or mute was often thought to be the work of a malicious spirit.

A pastor friend reading through the Gospel accounts of demon possession asked me if I believe in demons. My response was, "It's complicated." Here's why: In the Greco-Roman world, demons were thought to be the cause of nearly any physical or mental illness that defied the prevailing medical knowledge.

Recently I was in Italy and while there I repeatedly met people who seemed to be homeless and mentally ill. One was shouting at the sky. Another appeared to have been without a bath for some time and was bobbing her head up and down and whispering to herself. In the first century, most would have believed these people to be possessed by demons. Today, we recognize that these are often signs of mental illness or some kind of physical trauma or chemical imbalance.

Epilepsy is a prime example. In the first century, people commonly believed that epilepsy was the result of an attack of demons, or demon possession. This was true throughout most of the ancient world (and still is how epilepsy is understood in certain cultures today). On several occasions in the Bible, Jesus cast the demons out of those who seemed to be suffering from epilepsy.

No one in ancient times understood viruses or bacteria or the hypothalamus (the part of the brain where epilepsy seems to be centered). No one knew anything about schizophrenia or other conditions now routinely diagnosed as mental illness. How, otherwise, would we expect people in the ancient world to explain these conditions, except as the presence of demons?

So, was Jesus casting out demons or curing epilepsy? Was he healing mental illness or commanding evil spirits to flee? Perhaps he did both. To Jesus it did not seem important to distinguish between the two. He was bringing healing and deliverance. The people of his day did not understand the nature of epilepsy (we are still learning the physiological causes today) or many other diseases and forms of mental illness, and Jesus did not feel the need to explain what we would one day discover. He simply demonstrated the power of God by healing.

Demons in the Twenty-First Century

Today, when we use the term "demons" we are often talking about forces, influences, habits, or thoughts that lead us to do things that are destructive to ourselves or others. Several years ago I officiated at the funeral of a man who struggled his entire life with alcoholism. After drinking and driving he ran into a light pole, killing himself instantly. His friends said he had never been able to overcome the "demons" he struggled with. In that case they were talking not about disembodied spirits, but rather about the kind of spirits that come in a bottle and about the self-destructive forces that controlled him.

We routinely use the word today not only for addiction but for negative impulses such as the desire for revenge or lust or greed—things we know will bring pain but that we hope will somehow bring us relief.

What do we make of demons today? There are accounts of demonic activity that seem both supernatural and horrible. I don't dismiss the idea of spirits seeking to influence people in such ways. At the same time I'm hesitant to explain most things that happen in those terms. If we do so, where do we start and where do we stop? Using demons to explain those things removes personal responsibility and fails to recognize our advances in the fields of medical science and mental illness.

As I was writing this book, a young man walked into a high school in Ohio and began shooting. His girlfriend had broken up with him and started dating another boy. His attorneys claimed that he was having auditory hallucinations: he was hearing voices. Were the voices supernatural beings whispering in his ears? Or were they a form of mental illness? Or were they the kinds of voices from the dark side that all of us hear from time to time, urging us to do what we know is wrong and offering us a rationale for pursuing it?

During that same time period, an executive at a Fortune 100 company fell in love with a woman he worked with. Somewhere along the line he came to believe that he was supposed to kill the woman's husband, so that's just what he did. His defense was that an angel who looked like singer Olivia Newton-John told him to kill this man. Was the man suffering from schizophrenia? Was it a demon? Was it a fabrication, an attempt to be found not guilty by reason of insanity? As I told my friend the pastor, it's complicated.

As a pastor I've had two experiences with parishioners who believed they had seen or heard from demons. One had dabbled in the occult prior to her conversion to the Christian faith. The other had been serving God in Africa, in a community where curses and beliefs in spirits were not uncommon. For a time, both were plagued with experiences that were very real to them, were frightening, and seemed consistent with the demonic.

In each case I took seriously the possibility that the person was being oppressed by demons. I also recognized that there could be other possible causes that might be related to past traumatic experiences or to some physiological imbalance. To these individuals I said,

Yes, this could be demonic, and we're going to talk about that and what we can do to counter the demon if this is what you're being afflicted by. At the same time, let's consider other explanations that may require a different approach. In the end we want you free of these things, regardless of how the healing comes.

I encouraged them to see their doctors and share the experiences with them, and to consider seeing counselors as well.

I suggested that a three-pronged approach—doctor, counselor, pastor—would be the most holistic.

Ultimately I noted that my area of expertise is not physiological nor psychological, but spiritual. I referred them to the Gospel stories describing Jesus' power over the demons and reminded them that Jesus needed only to speak a word and the demons fled. I also reminded them that Jesus was never afraid of the demons, but they always were afraid of him. The passage we've just read, in which he cast out demons in the synagogue at Capernaum, is a perfect example. The demon, in crying out to Jesus, shows that it is afraid of being destroyed by him. What I find intriguing about these stories is that, as part of the encounter, usually the demon can't help but bear witness to Christ's identity. In the synagogue, where the demon would most wish to turn people from Jesus, it can't help but say, "You are the Holy One of God." So it is clear that Jesus has absolute power over the demons, and they know it.

Further, we noted how in the Scriptures those who followed Christ seemed to be able to claim the power of his name in dealing with demons. "You need to understand," I told my parishioners, "that it is not even a fair fight between Jesus and demons. His strength and power are infinitely greater than those of the forces of darkness. I want you to remember that!"

I encouraged them to read the Gospels before going to bed at night, perhaps starting with the stories of Jesus' power over the demons. (It was in the nighttime when these experiences occurred.) I encouraged them to pray and commit themselves to Christ before bed. I asked them to pray this way: "Jesus, I commit my life to you as I prepare to sleep. Hold me, protect me, and help me to sleep through the night." Then I made this suggestion: "After your prayer, speak to the demon, saying,

'Demon, if you are in this room, you've got to flee. I belong to Jesus Christ, and he is more powerful than you! In the name of Jesus Christ, be gone!'" I marked their foreheads with anointing oil in the sign of the cross, and I prayed for them. The practice of anointing, begun in Old Testament times, is a way of claiming something for God and invoking God's healing.

Both parishioners had had these experiences for long periods—one for months and one for years—but the experiences stopped after our time of prayer and their beginning to practice these things. Was it demon possession? Was it something psychological or spiritual? I don't know. I just know when we invoked the name of Jesus, it stopped.

Each of us hears voices at times calling us—the voice of the Spirit calling us to do right, the voice of darkness seeking to defeat us, destroy us, or simply lure us toward the darkness. We must decide which voice we will believe or follow. Following the voices on the dark side—the demons of revenge, jealousy, rage, addiction, fear, or suicidal thoughts—leads only to pain. Jesus, who is stronger than all those, said: "The thief comes only to steal and kill and destroy. I came that they may have life, and have it abundantly" (John 10:10 NRSV).

Jesus calls us to listen to *his* voice. He offers us life and has the power to make the demons flee.

Healing the Sick in Capernaum and Beyond

We've spoken of chasing out demons, but what of the healing miracles of Christ? There were hundreds of people healed by Jesus' touch in Capernaum.

One of my favorite healing stories involves a paralyzed man whose friends desperately wanted to take him to Jesus. The story is found in Mark 2, and it takes place at Capernaum, probably at Peter's house.

Based on excavations, Peter's home was a small place. If it had only one level, the home was approximately 625 square feet, with at least six adults living there. When Jesus taught in the house, there were hundreds who wanted to get in to catch a glimpse of him or to hear his voice. Crowds stood at the windows and the doors, spilling into the courtyard.

Several men had heard that Jesus was a healer. They had a friend who was sick, paralyzed, unable to walk. These men placed their friend on a stretcher, then picked him up and carried him to the house where Jesus was teaching. When they arrived, they found it impossible to get their friend inside to Jesus. So they improvised. They carried their friend up to the roof, which was made of thatch and mud, and began digging their way down, creating a large hole. I can almost hear Peter howling at these men as the dust and dried mud began to fall on the heads of Jesus and those closest to him. I picture Jesus stretching out his hand to still Peter and whispering, "Roofs can be repaired, Peter. But I want you to see this."

Using ropes, the men lowered the stretcher until their friend was lying in front of Jesus. Matthew, Mark, and Luke all say the same thing about what happened next: "Jesus, seeing their faith, said to the man, 'Your sins are forgiven. Get up. Take up your mat and walk'" (Mark 2:5-11, paraphrase). It's interesting to note that it wasn't the man's faith that got Jesus' attention. In fact, the man on the stretcher never said a word. We don't know if he had any faith. But his friends—who carried him, hoisted him onto the roof, tore the roof open, and lowered him to Jesus—they had faith! Because of *their* faith, Jesus healed the man.

There are several things we can take away from this story. The first is that all of us need stretcher-bearers. At the church I serve, we talk about this a lot. I ask our members regularly:

Who are the people who would pick you up, tear off the roof, and lower you to Jesus? We all need friends like that, whose faith is strong even when ours is weak, who are friends not just in word but in deed. These friendships don't just happen; you have to invest in them. Often the way this happens is through small groups in local churches—Sunday school classes, Bible studies, home-based groups. Who are our stretcher-bearers? Whose stretcher-bearers are you?

Second, it's important to realize the depth of Jesus' compassion for the sick. In every one of the Gospel healing stories, we find that Jesus made a point of noticing and then stopping to heal these sick people. He had both the power to heal and the compassion to use that power. He was constantly involved with people who were sick, blind, lame, deaf, dumb, and possessed, and he raised three people from the dead. He cared about the sick and troubled. It is vital to know and remember that when you are sick, Jesus notices. He has compassion. He is concerned. That is the kind of God we serve.

Third, it appears that the paralyzed man's malady was spiritual and psychological, not physical. The problem wasn't his spinal cord; it was his heart. Jesus said, "Your sins are forgiven" and only then added, "Take up your mat and walk." Perhaps the man was paralyzed with guilt over something he had done in the past. I have seen this before with people in my own congregation. Jesus in essence was saying, "I know the thing that has bound you, and I have authority to say this to you: 'You are forgiven. Get up and walk.'"

As I read these words, I think of a man I knew who was overcome with guilt over the death of his daughter. A few hours after he had verbally snapped at her during a conversation, she took her own life. The last words he ever spoke to her were in the heat of conflict. After that, he carried a paralyzing guilt that if only he had not said those words, she would still be alive. Others tried to tell him that her suicide wasn't caused by his remarks, but he was unconvinced. For years he was overwhelmed, paralyzed emotionally and spiritually, until finally he was able to trust in the grace of Christ and to hear the words "Your sins are forgiven." At that point, on an emotional level, he could walk again.

Not long ago I was praying for someone, anointing her in the front of the church, when she said, "I'm like that man in the Bible who was paralyzed. I feel so overwhelmed with guilt, and I can't believe that God would forgive me. Would you please pray for me?" After I had anointed her, I said, "Would you look at me for a moment? Just this moment I feel that God wants me to tell you exactly what Jesus said to the man who was paralyzed. I think God wants you to hear this. Your sins are forgiven. Take up your mat and walk."

In the house at Capernaum, Jesus healed the man's heart, which led to his physical recovery. Jesus still heals hearts. He still forgives sins. He still heals our bodies, casts out demons, and sets people free. And we still need stretcher-bearers, people who will carry us and pray for us and have faith for us, when our own faith is weak or nonexistent.

You may ask, "What about physical healing? We know he heals us spiritually. But does he heal us physically, even today?"

I've spent the last couple of months on my knees twice a day praying for Joyce, a woman in our congregation whom I dearly love. I've been her pastor for seventeen years. She has just been diagnosed with cancer throughout her body. Joyce has always been a pillar of strength for others. She and her husband are key leaders in our church. Though I know better, I've even bargained with God: "Lord, what can I give you in exchange for her healing? I would give you anything if you would make her better."

I met with Joyce and her husband after the doctors had given them very little hope. I told them how much I loved them and acknowledged the gravity of the news, then said to them:

The doctors can tell us what typically happens, and what you might expect. It is important to take this seriously. We're going to pray that God will give the doctors wisdom and help them to be his instruments. We'll do this because when God wants something done on the earth, he typically uses people. Doctors, nurses, and medical professionals are his ordinary means of working for healing today.

Your mind and body are also equipped with tremendous healing power that we don't fully understand. So I'm going to invite you to trust God with your life and to pray that God will strengthen and work through your body's systems that fight off disease.

We're also going to pray for a miracle—for God to intervene and bring healing to your body. I've prayed for people who were healed in ways the doctors could not explain. And I've also prayed for people who were not healed. God's ordinary ways of working are through doctors, nurses, hospitals, and medicine. But at times, for reasons I can't fully explain, I've seen miracles happen and so we're going to pray for this.

I don't believe God gave you this cancer, any more than you would inject cancer cells into your children's bodies. But I do believe God can bring good from this and be at work through you in the midst of your battle with cancer. Ultimately, none of us knows what the future holds, but we do know that no matter what, God will not let you go. You belong to him, Joyce.

As I write this, Joyce and her husband are still fighting the battle. Joyce has laid out her funeral plans, "just in case." Yet she is fighting with all the tools at her disposal: a positive attitude, stretcher-bearers from her small group and church, great doctors, lots of hope, prayers for a miracle, trust that if a miracle does not happen she will be okay in the hands of her Lord, and the conviction that "the worst thing is never the last thing."

Maybe now you can see why I say it's complicated. John, in his Gospel, calls Jesus' miracles "signs." They are acts of power that lead to something more profound. They tell us about Jesus' identity, and they teach us about the gospel. They point toward the ultimate healing that will take place in the Kingdom, and to the spiritual healing that Jesus works here and now.

Walking in Christ's Footsteps

This book is about walking in the footsteps of Jesus, not just in the Holy Land but in our daily lives. If Christ set the oppressed free, delivered people from their demons, and brought healing to the sick and wounded, what does that mean for us as his followers?

As I told Joyce and her husband, God most often uses people to accomplish his work. How grateful I am today for therapists and doctors, friends and family, believers individually and the entire church. All of them—and all of us—are instruments that God uses to deliver and heal. At one point Oral Roberts, who made his name as a travelling faith healer, started a university. It seemed like a strange thing for a faith healer to do. But Oral came to believe that God works through ordinary people who become instruments of healing. He believed doctors and lawyers and school teachers and scientists were all instruments of God's healing. I appreciate that idea.

When doctors, nurses, and ordinary folks from the congregation I serve go to Haiti, Honduras, and various countries in Africa to staff medical clinics, they go as God's hands. They become instruments of healing. When leaders in our recovery ministries befriend and support those who are leaving behind addictions, they become instruments of deliverance. When church friends surround a member of their small group with prayer during illness or make hospital visits to offer encouragement and love, they are walking in the footsteps of Jesus in helping with the healing process. We are all called to be healers.

Jesus was constantly looking for the sick and oppressed. He had a heart for them. This is what we see as he stayed up all night at Peter's home to heal the sick and cast out demons. There are people all around us who are sick or oppressed. If you walk in the footsteps of Jesus, you look for them; you seek to be instruments of God's healing and deliverance.

Whose stretcher-bearer are you?

Reflection
Restored to Life

When they came to the house of the leader of the synagogue, he saw a commotion, people weeping and wailing
loudly. When he had entered, he said to them, "Why do you
make a commotion and weep? The child is not dead but
sleeping." And they laughed at him. Then he put them all
outside, and took the child's father and mother and those
who were with him, and went in where the child was. He
took her by the hand and said to her, "Talitha cum," which
means, "Little girl, get up!" And immediately the girl got up
and began to walk about (she was twelve years of age).

(Mark 5:38-42 NRSV)

In today's story, the lay leader of the synagogue was a
man named Jairus. His twelve-year-old daughter was very
sick at home, and he had fallen at Jesus' feet, begging Jesus
to come and heal his daughter. Jesus immediately left with
Jairus, but while they were on the way home, friends came
to say that the daughter had died. Jesus turned to Jairus
and said, "Do not fear, only believe" (Mark 5:36 NRSV).

Jesus took Jairus, his wife, and a few disciples to the
girl's room and asked the mourners to leave. He took the
girl by the hand and spoke, commanding her to get up, and
immediately she was well! What a remarkable scene.

This was the second instance in the Gospels of Jesus
restoring someone to life. The first, recorded in Luke 7:11-
17, took place in a town called Nain, where Jesus had seen

a widow grieving the death of her son. His heart had gone out to the widow, and he had stopped the funeral procession, saying to her dead son, "Young man, get up!" The boy sat up, very much alive (Luke 7:14-15).

A third incident of Jesus raising someone from the grave is found in John 11, where Jesus was moved to tears at the grief of Lazarus' sister. Jesus went to the tomb and shouted, "Lazarus, come out!" To everyone's astonishment, Lazarus stumbled out of the grave (John 11:43-44).

These stories have two things in common. First, in each instance Jesus was moved with compassion for those who were grieving. He knew that on the other side of death was life, and that those who have died live again; nevertheless, he was deeply moved by the sorrow of those who mourned. Second, Jesus spoke to the people who had died, and by his word their bodies were reanimated. The biochemical processes of death and decay were instantly reversed, and their souls reentered their bodies—all at the sound of his voice.

Some years ago, a twelve-year-old girl in our congregation named Katie died of a rare disease. Her mother and father, like Jairus and his wife, loved their daughter very much. I shared this story from Mark's gospel at Katie's funeral. It served as a reminder of Christ's compassion for grieving parents. But this story, and the other stories of resurrection in the Gospels, point to the hope we have in Christ. Katie died at 8:30 a.m. on a Sunday morning. I'm convinced that on that day, at that very hour, Jesus said to her, *"Talitha cum"* ("Little girl, get up!").

Jesus is deeply moved by our grief. And he is "the resurrection and the life." Those who believe in him, "though they die, yet shall they live." In the words of Charles Wesley's famous hymn, "He speaks, and listening to his voice, new life the dead receive!"*

Lord, I remember now those whom I have loved and lost to death. Thank you for the Gospel stories in which you spoke and people rose to life. I trust that my loved ones are with you and that one day I will see you, and them, face to face. Amen.

* Charles Wesley, "O For a Thousand Tongues to Sing," *The United Methodist Hymnal* (Nashville: The United Methodist Publishing House, 1989), 57.

From *The Way: 40 Days of Reflection*. Abingdon Press, 2012.

Sea of Galilee at ancient harbor of Capernaum

Main hall of synagogue, Capernaum

Simon Peter's house, Capernaum

Mills and presses, Capernaum

PALESTINE
AT THE TIME
OF JESUS

3. Proclaiming the Kingdom
The Mountains

When Jesus saw the crowds, he went up the mountain; and after he sat down, his disciples came to him. Then he began to speak, and taught them....

Matthew 5:1-2a NRSV

"Everyone then who hears these words of mine and acts on them will be like a wise man who built his house on rock. The rain fell, the floods came, and the winds blew and beat on that house, but it did not fall, because it had been founded on rock. And everyone who hears these words of mine and does not act on them will be like a foolish man who built his house on sand. The rain fell, and the floods came, and the winds blew and beat against that house, and it fell—and great was its fall!" Now when Jesus had finished saying these things, the crowds were astounded at his teaching, for he taught them as one having authority, and not as their scribes.

Matthew 7:24-29 NRSV

MOUNTAINS PROVIDE THE SETTING FOR many of the most dramatic and memorable stories in the Old and New Testaments. Abraham heard the voice of God while preparing to sacrifice Isaac on Mt. Moriah. Moses was at Mt. Horeb when he saw the burning bush. David wrote many of his psalms from the mountains of the Judean wilderness. Elijah heard the voice of God while on the mountain. And Jesus was drawn to the mountains.

James Ridgeway Sr., a retired United Methodist pastor and founder of Educational Opportunities, a non-profit organization that takes people on tours of the Holy Land, once told me that you could tell most of Jesus' story by speaking of mountains. Dr. Ridgeway, who had been to the Holy Land more than one hundred times, then proceeded to tell Jesus' story through the lens of the mountains:

Following his baptism Jesus was tempted on a mountain. Upon his entrance into Galilee he prayed all night on a mountain and then chose his disciples. He gave his best-known sermon on the mount. He multiplied the loaves and fish on a mountainside. When Jesus was tired he went up on the mountains to pray by himself. He healed the sick on the mountain. While praying with Peter, James, and John on a mountain, he was transfigured, and Moses and Elijah appeared to him. Jesus entered Jerusalem for the last week of his life from the Mount of Olives. He returned there to pray each night. He was arrested on the Mount of Olives, was taken to Mt. Zion to be tried before the Sanhedrin, was tortured by Pilate and then crucified on Mt. Calvary (a hill that was itself a part of the greater Mt. Zion). After his resurrection he gave the great commission from a mountain, where he ascended to heaven.

Clearly the mountains were important to Jesus.

It is easy to understand Jesus' connection to the mountains. When I ask people where they feel closest to God, I typically hear three answers: church, the mountains, and a lake or ocean. Jesus went to the mountains to pray and to connect with God. When I'm emotionally or spiritually depleted, my wife LaVon will say to me, "Why don't you take some time and get away to walk and pray?" She has said to me, "If Jesus needed to take time away to think and pray, who do you think you are that you don't need it?"

I've found that even a few hours away devoted to prayer, reading, and reflection clears my head, improves my creativity, and renews my vision for ministry. Twenty-four hours away has a huge impact for me. Regardless of your line of work, whether you stay at home and constantly give to your kids and neighbors, or whether you're going a hundred miles an hour as an executive, you've got to find time to get away, to renew, and to refresh your connection with God. If you walk in the footsteps of Jesus, you'll spend regular periods of time alone on your own mountain, wherever it may be, in prayer and meditation.

How Jesus Taught

Jesus didn't just pray on the mountain; he also taught there. The most influential "sermon" in Western civilization is the one Jesus gave as he went up on a mountain and began to teach his disciples. In this chapter we'll consider what Jesus taught in the Sermon on the Mount. But before we do, I'd like to think with you for a moment about *how* Jesus taught.

We tend to read the words of Jesus as though he were a twenty-first-century teacher in the Western world, where we prefer teachers to give us the facts, speak in a straightforward manner, make linear arguments, and generally intend for what

A Land of Contrasts

The geology of the Holy Land is fascinating. For such a small country (only 263 miles from north to south and only 71 miles across at its widest point) there is great diversity in geological forms. Its location as the bridge between Eurasia and Africa, along with the movement of the earth's tectonic plates in that region, produced an amazing array of ecosystems.

To the north are mountains formed of volcanic activity millions of years ago. Most ancient Near Eastern villages were constructed of black basalt produced by those volcanoes. Mt. Hermon, far to the north, is snowcapped and attracts skiers. It is roughly nine thousand feet tall. The Galilee region is made up of many rolling hills and mountains, from 1,000 to 3,500 feet tall. This region is the breadbasket of the country, with crops and forests everywhere. It is also home to the Sea of Galilee, the largest freshwater body in the Holy Land and the lowest freshwater body on earth.

As you move to the south, the climate and rainfall levels change dramatically. South of the Galilee region is what in Jesus' time was known as Samaria, and which today is known as the West Bank. It is a transitional zone, half of which is still quite fertile with millions of olive trees and vast areas under cultivation. But the southern end of the West Bank becomes much more mountainous and arid, and there you're more likely to see Bedouin shepherds with their flocks, or herds of camel, than farmers.

South of Jerusalem the country becomes a desert of amazing beauty with mountains and valleys and ravines. At this end of the country is the Dead Sea, the lowest body of water of any kind on the planet. The Sea of Galilee and the Dead Sea are sixty-five miles apart, but what a difference that sixty-five miles makes. The two are linked by the Jordan River, which twists and turns its way from the north to the south. This entire region of the Holy Land is a part of the Jordan Rift Valley. Beyond the Dead Sea is the vast Negev, the desert that comprises over half of modern Israel's land mass. The desert continues to the south where, at a narrow point, it connects with the Red Sea at the resort town of Eliat.

Most of Jesus' public ministry took place around the Sea of Galilee. When the Gospels refer to Jesus going to the mountains these were typically one thousand to three thousand feet in height, covered with grasses or crops with occasional cliffs and caves where he might have spent the night.

they say to be taken fairly literally. But Jesus was a first-century Jewish teacher in the Eastern world. In that time and in that part of the world, teachers told stories to convey truth. They made frequent use of analogy. And they used figures of speech to make their point and to help people remember it. Jesus drew metaphors and stories from the everyday lives and experiences of first-century farmers, shepherds, and fishermen.

Despite this difference in teaching style, Jesus' words typically make sense even to the uninitiated—not to all of them, perhaps, but to most of them. I came to be a follower of Jesus after reading through the first three Gospels. I was fourteen years old and began with Matthew's Gospel, several chapters a night. By the time I finished Luke's Gospel, I knew I wanted to follow Jesus. Since then I've read the Gospels over and over again, and my understanding of Jesus' words has changed and deepened. But thirty-four years later, as I read his words and his story, I want more than ever to follow him and to be the person he describes in the Gospels.

There are several things I have learned about how Jesus taught that have helped me understand his words. Many people, not knowing these things, find themselves frustrated. I will mention three tips that will help you as you read the words of Jesus.

First, Jesus nearly always spoke using figures of speech. In his daily life this may not have been so, but what is recorded in the Gospels relies heavily upon the use of analogies including similes and parables. Similes, as you may recall from high school English, are comparisons usually using the words *like* or *as*. Jesus frequently said things such as "The kingdom of God is like..." and then told of some commonplace concept, often from agriculture, so that he could make the complex understandable.

I love this about Jesus. It's been said that modern preachers take the simple and make it confusing, but that Jesus took the confusing and made it easy to understand. The challenge with figures of speech is that the comparisons are not exact, and there are a thousand ways in which *this* is not like *that*. So, comparisons break down—they cannot be pushed too far. Nevertheless, figures of speech can be very helpful in making sense of complex things or in teaching an important theological, ethical, or spiritual point. We do need to keep in mind, of course, that we live two thousand years later in a very different world, so some of the comparisons are not as easily understood as they were to Jesus' first hearers.

Second, Jesus spoke in parables. Parables are short, vivid, easy-to-remember stories intended to illustrate spiritual truths. Some of Jesus' parables were extended similes that added some form of action to the simile. (The Parable of the Mustard Seed is an example.) The Good Samaritan, the Prodigal Son, Lazarus and the Rich Man, and the Sheep and the Goats are some of Jesus' best-known parables, and each tells us something about God, our neighbors, judgment, or some other important concept. This way of teaching with stories was thoroughly Jewish. Some of Jesus' parables were easily understood by nearly anyone paying attention; some required more thought and produced additional insights the more one thought about it.

Not only did similes and parables make complex ideas clear to ordinary people; they had the added benefit of being easily remembered. Any preacher will tell you that while the "meat" of the sermon is what matters most, the stories used to illustrate it are what people will remember.

Third, Jesus spoke using a technique that some have called "prophetic hyperbole." Understanding this technique was very helpful to me in making sense of the things Jesus taught. To speak prophetically is to speak boldly in broad terms, without attempting to identify or address exceptions to the rule. (There are almost always exceptions to the rule that justify its breaking.)[6] Hyperbole is a figure of speech that exaggerates to the point of the absurd in order to make a point. Examples from everyday speech include "I'm so hungry I could eat a horse," "These shoes are killing me," and "I've told you a million times."

Consider these words of Jesus that deploy prophetic hyperbole: "If your eye causes you to sin, pluck it out. If your hand causes you to sin, cut it off." Over the years there have been Christians who literally maimed themselves attempting to follow Jesus' words. His point, though, was not that we should harm ourselves, but that sin is dangerous; take it seriously. Jesus also said: "It's harder for a rich man to enter the kingdom of Heaven than it is for a camel to pass through the eye of a needle." He was speaking in prophetic hyperbole—riches can destroy your soul.[7] There were many other places in Scripture where Jesus spoke in prophetic hyperbole. We are meant to take what he said seriously, but we get in trouble at times when we take it literally.

Understanding a few things about *how* Jesus taught, we'll now consider briefly *what* Jesus taught. Then we'll climb the mountain with him to consider how his Sermon on the Mount might speak to us today. We'll close by considering the two great commandments as a summary of all that Jesus taught.

The Central Focus of Jesus' Message:
The Kingdom of God

Many Christians and Christian churches emphasize the necessity of having a "personal relationship with Jesus Christ" as the locus of the Christian life. I agree that this is a powerful and very important part of faith. But if you read the Gospels, particularly Matthew, Mark, and Luke, you'll find that Jesus spoke very little about this idea. He was more concerned about inviting people to become his followers and to live according to the way he laid out for them. When Jesus approached the fishermen on the seashore, he did not say, "Accept me into your hearts." He said, "Come and follow me."

I mention this not to downplay the importance of a personal relationship with Jesus, but to invite us to take seriously what he actually said in the Gospels. The central focus of Jesus' preaching and teaching was on doing the will of God, and on something he referred to as the kingdom of God (or the kingdom of heaven). He spoke of it more than forgiveness, sin, and even love *combined*. He mentioned the Kingdom over one hundred times, largely in Matthew, Mark, and Luke, but also implicitly in John. Mark recounts Jesus' earliest message thus: "Jesus went to Galilee proclaiming the good news of God. 'The time has come,' he said. 'The kingdom of God is near; repent, and believe the good news'" (Mark 1:14b-15 NIV).

What did Jesus mean by the kingdom of God? Entire books have been filled trying to answer that question. Most authorities agree that the essential idea is that God is the rightful ruler of the entire universe. God is King, and all creation owes its existence to him. He is the Creator of all things. He is the Sustainer of the universe. To be a part of God's kingdom is to recognize his kingship and to seek to live according to his will.

There were three senses in which Jesus spoke about the kingdom of God. The Kingdom is, first, a present reality, and we can choose to become a part of it by yielding our lives to the King. When we repent (that is, return to God's kingdom and path) we pledge to love, honor, and serve our King by doing his will. And we find, in the words of St. Augustine, that "in his will is our peace." As we do his will, our lives change. Everything we touch is affected by our citizenship in the Kingdom.

In this first sense, the Kingdom grows with each person who yields to God as King. It starts small, like a mustard seed, but as one person and then two and then three come to faith, share their faith, and live by that faith, the Kingdom begins to change entire communities and ultimately the entire world.

Second, the kingdom of God is a vision. Some might say it is Jesus' utopian vision of what our lives and the world would look like if God's will were done on earth. Much of Jesus' teaching, particularly in the Sermon on the Mount, was focused on laying out the ideals of the Kingdom. We may never, this side of heaven, fully live up to those ideals, but we strive for them daily.

And when entire communities live this way we begin to see the world as God intended it to be.

Finally, the kingdom of God is something that is yet to be. Jesus taught that there would come a day when, in the words of Revelation (as adapted by Handel), "the kingdom of this world is become the kingdom of our Lord, and of his Christ; and he shall reign forever and ever. Hallelujah!" Jesus taught that there will come a final judgment day when the world as we know it will be drawn to a close and there will be a new heaven and a new earth. God's kingdom will finally come on earth as it is in heaven.

One last word about the kingdom of God: much of what Jesus said in his teaching was given in the plural—in other words, his commands were to be lived out in community. The church is meant to be a foreshadowing of the future kingdom. It is meant to be, in a sense, a foreign embassy wherever it is located. And when we look at the church, we're meant to experience at least a foretaste of what the future kingdom will be like—people who belong to God, who love and trust God, and who seek together to do God's will.

The New Law for the Kingdom of God

Matthew writes, "When Jesus saw the crowds, he went up the mountain; and after he sat down, his disciples came to him. Then he began to speak, and taught them" (Matthew 5:1-2 NRSV).

This image of Jesus going up on the mountain to teach is intended by Matthew to remind us of Moses, who ascended Mt. Sinai and there received the law from God. Jesus went up on the mountain, and there he delivered the new law. Jesus is pictured as the new Moses giving the new law, not merely for the nation of Israel but for the kingdom of God, a kingdom that transcends all earthly boundaries.

In light of everything we've considered, let's examine the message that Jesus gave to the crowds that day on the mountain.[8] I would encourage you to have your Bible open to Matthew 5-7 as we briefly walk through the Sermon on the Mount.

The Beatitudes
Matthew 5:1-12

"Blessed are the poor in spirit, for theirs is the kingdom of heaven..." (Matthew 5:3 NRSV). With these words Jesus began his magnificent message, and he immediately followed it with seven more statements that begin, "Blessed are the..." We call these the Beatitudes, from the Latin word for "blessed." Let's consider this first Beatitude in detail.

The word "blessed" is actually, in this context, a commendation and word of encouragement to people who otherwise might feel defeated and discouraged about the coming of better days. These people are to consider themselves fortunate or happy because they have already been credited with a gift from God, though they will not see it until they see the Kingdom fully come.

"Blessed are the poor in spirit." Who are the poor in spirit? The phrase can mean those who are pushed down and made to feel small by the world around them—they are the humbled. But it can also mean those who humble themselves before God. What it definitely does not include is the proud and the arrogant. The poor in spirit are fortunate because the kingdom of God, now and in the future, belongs to them. Job 5:11, Proverbs 3:34, and James 4:10 capture the same idea, one that permeates Scripture, that God humbles the arrogant and lifts up the lowly.

The Beatitudes—this first one and the remaining seven— point to what some call the Great Reversal: Those who seem to have it all together, who today are on top, will find in the future dimension of the Kingdom that they will be on the bottom. Elsewhere in the Gospels, Jesus says it another way: The first shall be last and the last shall be first.

This and the other Beatitudes not only speak words of encouragement to the poor in spirit; they also are meant to move the arrogant to humility. The Beatitudes encourage and they call. This first Beatitude reminds me of Jesus' words when he taught his disciples: "The greatest among you will be your servant. All who exalt themselves will be humbled, and all who humble themselves will be exalted" (Matthew 23:11-12 NRSV).

Read the rest of the Beatitudes. See which ones encourage you and which ones call you. As you read them, consider what Jesus was saying, not only about the future kingdom, but also about living as citizens of his kingdom today.

The Mission of God's People: Beautiful Deeds
Matthew 5:13-16

It is important to note that immediately after his statement of encouragement and call, Jesus laid out the mission of God's people. If you are a citizen of the Kingdom, then you have a mission. Today it is common to hear people speak of the "missional church," and I'm grateful for it; but there is not, nor has there ever been, an authentic church nor Christian who was not "missional." I love Paul's words in Ephesians 2:10, where he writes, "For we are what he has made us, created in Christ Jesus for good works, which God prepared beforehand to be our way of life" (NRSV). We were created for good works—for missional living!

In this passage from the Sermon on the Mount, Jesus offered two powerful metaphors for those who serve God as King. In the first metaphor, Jesus said to his disciples, "You are the salt of the earth." Salt was used then, as now, to season food, to bring out the best flavor in whatever it touched. It was also a preservative, to keep food from spoiling. I love this image. Everything we touch should be improved by the encounter, even as we help preserve the good of God's creation.

I knew a man who took this role seriously. In every encounter throughout the day, he tried to leave people uplifted or encouraged. He would constantly leave notes for people, writing things such as "Thank you," or "Well done," or "I really appreciate that about you." To make sure the notes didn't seem inauthentic, he worked on offering specific and honest words of encouragement; otherwise sometimes he simply offered smiles. When he could do a kind deed for someone, he did. He woke up each day seeing this as his mission. He served God as King, and he was shaking salt on all that he encountered.

In the second metaphor, Jesus said, "You are the light of the world. A city built on a hill cannot be hid" (Matthew 5:14 NRSV). What a powerful picture of our mission as God's people! I've found this idea powerfully illustrated when sitting on the hillsides of the Sea of Galilee at night, watching the lights. In Jesus' day there were a number of villages on these hillsides, and even then, with only oil lamps, one could watch the sun set over the Galilee and see the village lights across the lake, which truly could not be hidden.

Jesus' words echoed a part of the mission God had given to Israel: to be a "light for the Gentiles, to open the eyes that are blind" (Isaiah 42:6-7 NIV). How are we to serve as light? Jesus said, "Let your light shine before others, so that they may see your good works and give glory to your Father in heaven" (Matthew 5:16 NRSV).

89

These are our daily marching orders, and the word choice is interesting. There are several Greek words for "good," but the word used in "good deeds" is *kallos*. More than just "good," this word means "beautiful" or "winsome." Our deeds are meant be so attractive that others are naturally drawn to the God we serve.

Are your deeds winsome and beautiful to others? There are enough Christians today whose attitudes seem judgmental and uncharitable to those around them. Don't be one of those Christians. Instead may your life, and our churches, be characterized by beautiful deeds, flowing from hearts of compassion and love that draw others into the Kingdom.

Exercises in Remembering the Point
Matthew 5:17-48

In the final section of Matthew 5, Jesus spoke of, and reinterpreted, some of the commandments in the Law of Moses. What he knew and addressed elsewhere in the Gospels was that many people obeyed the letter of the Law but missed its intent.

Anyone who has ever raised children can appreciate the difference. You tell your kids they have to be in bed, lights out, by ten o'clock on a school night, but two hours later you go upstairs and they are talking on the phone while playing games on an iPad. You ask, "What part of 'lights out' and 'in bed' did you not understand?" They answer, "But Dad, I am in bed with the lights out!"

Yet Jesus set an even higher standard. He called people to consider the intent of the commands, but also to seek a righteousness that went beyond the Law and instead to God's original intent for humanity. Let's take a quick look at the six commandments he addressed, along with his responses. Please follow along in your own Bible, as this list is abbreviated:

- The Law says, "Don't murder."
  I say, "Don't even insult your neighbor."
- The Law says, "Don't commit adultery."
  I say, "Don't look with lust at another."
- The Law says, "You can divorce."[9]
  I say, "Don't leave your spouse."[10]
- The Law says, "Don't swear falsely."
  I say, "Do what you say you'll do."
- The Law says, "An eye for an eye."
  I say, "Turn the other cheek."
- The Law says, "Love your neighbor."
  I say, "Love your enemy."

Some might read this and say, "I thought Christianity was about grace and forgiveness. Jesus just made things harder than Moses and the Law did! Yes, and yes. Remember the kingdom of God is the ideal. It is what God intended for humanity.

Jesus gave these responses as examples; I'm not sure they are exhaustive. At points they seem impossible, but I see them as the ideal I wish to strive for. When human beings live with this ideal in mind, so much of the pain we see in our world gives way to peace.

Here's just one example: How much different would our national and local elections be if all who claimed to be Christ followers, including those running for office, actually practiced Matthew 5:21-26 on insulting others, Matthew 5:35-37 about keeping promises, and 5:43-47 on loving our enemies?

It's not just the candidates and their campaigns that would benefit from doing as Jesus taught. At times the media voices foster fear and distrust, defame character, and help mobilize the base on both the left and the right. Many a Christian has done the same by forwarding e-mails without checking the facts—e-mails sure to inflame but not guaranteed to be true. If, before and after voting day, all the Americans who say they are Christ followers actually carried out Jesus' teachings, imagine how different our elections and election-year politics would be.

Practicing Acts of Personal Piety
Matthew 6:1-18

In Matthew 6, Jesus made it clear that we often do the right thing for the wrong reason.

Jesus noted that the religious leaders practiced their piety in such a way as to be noticed by others. He said, in essence, "They pray and fast and help the poor, but they do it so people will notice and praise them." Jesus taught that if his hearers did those same things in secret, so that others might not see, then their acts would truly be for God or for those who might receive the gifts. He taught, in other words, that our motives are as important as our actions, which was the very point he was making in Matthew 5, when he reinterpreted the Law of Moses.

I suspect that all of us have been guilty at some time or other of doing good in order to be noticed. When we give to charitable organizations, do we agree to have our names listed among the donors? How often do we give because we feel the need for people to know about it?

When we fast at Lent, do we let people know we're fasting and tell them how hard it is to give something up for forty days? If you gave up something for Lent, how many people did you tell?

And when we've taken time to pray, are we quick to report on what we did? Why would we tell others?

I think it's normal to want affirmation when we do things that are good and noble. But the ideal, and what we strive for as we grow in our faith, is to do these things in secret as an offering to God or, in the case of helping others, simply for the sake of helping them. Those with real spiritual maturity don't look for a reward, except for the knowledge that someone was helped through their donation, that God heard the cries of their heart during Lent, or that their prayers opened them to God's Spirit.

Occasionally I catch some of these more mature disciples "in the act." Some time ago I walked into the chapel of our church and saw one of our leaders, a man who I know is also a leader in his industry, kneeling alone in prayer. Concerned that something might be wrong, I waited until he was finished and asked, "Is everything okay?" "Yes," he replied. "I just felt drawn to spend time in conversation with God today." There was a woman who routinely, when hearing about the needs of individuals in our church, would slip cash to one of the associate pastors to distribute to the individuals anonymously. She was afraid to send cash through the mail, and she didn't want to use a check because the person would see her name on it.

Do you ever struggle with this teaching of Jesus? I do at times. But the Sermon on the Mount gives me God's vision of the ideal, and so in my acts of piety I work to suppress the need to be noticed and to cultivate the discipline of invisibility. By the way, I take comfort from the fact that half a chapter of Matthew is devoted to this. It must mean that others struggle with it as well!

One last note about this section of the Sermon on the Mount: Don't miss the chance to pause and use the pattern prayer Jesus offered here—what we call the Lord's Prayer. But don't say it too fast. Each phrase is pregnant with meaning, and at any point in the prayer it is appropriate to expand upon its content. Notice especially Jesus' words about forgiveness and the importance of mercy in the kingdom of God.

Money, Possessions, and Worry
Matthew 6:19-34

Matthew 6 ends with Jesus addressing questions of our relationship with money and possessions, and the issue of our worry about them. Jesus' words remind me that the more things change, the more they stay the same. As simple as their lives were, first-century shepherds, farmers, and fishermen seem also to have struggled with materialism and their desire for more.

We constantly must be reminded of Jesus' statement that we cannot have two masters. We must choose: is God King, or is cash king? In my family, the only way we've been able to make the right choice is by committing to give God the first part of our earnings. My wife LaVon and I married right out of high school, and I immediately went to college. We lived below the poverty level that first year, but we committed to give to God the first tenth of our income. The idea of the tithe comes from Abraham's time, when 10 percent was "the king's portion." Our tithe is another way of recognizing that God is our King. As our income grew, LaVon and I set a goal of giving away an increasing percentage of our income every year—the first tenth to God's work through our church, and beyond that to missions and ministries benefiting the poor.

Jesus said not to store up treasure. He repeated this elsewhere in the Gospels. Here again, it becomes important to understand Jesus' use of prophetic hyperbole, as well as the historical context. In the first century, families lived together. When elderly members of the family could not work anymore, they rested, and the work of tending the sheep or tilling the soil was continued by the other family members. They didn't need to "store up treasure" for retirement, because they had children or family to live with. Our society, on so many different levels, doesn't work this way. Saving for retirement is a responsibility, not a luxury, and so we set aside some of our income to provide for our needs when we can no longer work.

Yet we still struggle with how much is enough, and for many of us our 401K retirement account becomes a golden calf. Here's a little test: Which do you do more: pray or check your stock values? Which do you think about more: God's vision for your future or your vision for retirement? How easily our plans and our retirement money become idols, drawing our heart and attention away from God. One of my favorite parables of Jesus is the Rich Fool, in Luke 12:13-21, especially verse 15: "Take care! Be on your guard against all kinds of greed; for one's life does not consist in the abundance of possessions" (NRSV).

Why did Jesus have to say this? Because even in the first century, peasants in Palestine were tempted to believe that their lives could be measured by the abundance of their possessions. If they were tempted to believe this, how much more are we, who are bombarded with dozens (hundreds!) of e-mail, radio, television, and pop-up ads each day, shouting at us that we'll finally be happy if we have the latest gadget, drive the latest car, or wear the latest styles.

For those of you who are people of some means, you probably have figured out that there comes a point where the amount you have left after tithing and appropriately funding your retirement is far more than what you need to live. If so, you have a couple of choices: you can raise your standard of living, or you can raise your standard of giving.

A family I know locked in their standard of living about ten years ago. He was a fellow writer, and over the last ten years his income grew as more and more people purchased his books. As his income grew, he was finally able to save for retirement as he had hoped, but he saw that the real opportunity was to raise his standard of giving. He had already been a generous person, tithing and giving beyond that the tithe. But he and his wife began setting aside a third of their after-tax income to give away. At the end of ten years, they had saved enough to do a few things for themselves, but their priority continued to be giving. Another family I know—a doctor and his wife–gives away half of all they have to serve the King and his kingdom.

Many of us have the opposite problem. We worry constantly that we don't have enough. For those of us living in the developed world, I'm confident about what Jesus said in Matthew 6:25-34—don't worry, and you'll have enough to eat and drink and wear. Of course, I don't think he meant that we should just lie around, and food will appear at our door. We work, we focus, we may have to downsize, but somehow we'll eat, and we'll have clothes on our back and shoes on our feet. This was true in first-century Palestine, too.

But what about those who live in the developing world, in regions where drought can leave hundreds of thousands of people without food to eat? It is here I am reminded that the way God provides for the needs of the "least of these" is through those with more than enough. This is precisely what John the Baptist was preaching and what Jesus was describing in the parables of Lazarus and the Rich Man, the Good Samaritan, and the Sheep and the Goats.

For those of us in the developed world, Jesus' words are an opportunity to consider how God meets the needs of the poor, but also a reminder that worrying won't add an inch to our height or a day to our life. I do my part; God does his part. My task, when it comes to money and possessions, is to "strive first for the kingdom of God and his righteousness, and all these things will be given to you as well" (Matthew 6:33 NRSV).

No Judging Others, Do Unto Others, A Wise Builder
Matthew 7

It is easy when reading Matthew 5 and 6 to think of people you know in the church who don't live according to Jesus' words. There is the woman who routinely calls people "Idiot!" while driving down the road. There is that person who serves Communion who you know is not very grace-filled. There is the guy in your row at church who, when the offering plate is passed, always puts his check facing upward and writes in extra-large print, so everyone can see how much he gave that week. There are the divorced Christians and the guy who you heard has struggled with pornography. Then there is the preacher who just bought a black Mustang convertible that goes zero to sixty in 4.3 seconds. Clearly that preacher needs to read the Sermon on the Mount again.

About the time you're thinking these things, you come to Matthew 7:1-5:

> "Do not judge, so that you may not be judged. For with the judgment you make you will be judged, and the measure you give will be the measure you get. Why do you see the speck in your neighbor's eye, but do not notice the log in your own eye? Or how can you say to your neighbor, 'Let me take the speck out of your eye,' while the log is in your own eye? You hypocrite, first take the log out of your own eye, and then you will see clearly to take the speck out of your neighbor's eye." (NRSV)

Ouch.

This passage isn't about someone else. It's about you and me. In God's kingdom, we give others the benefit of the doubt and focus on our own issues rather than pointing to others. (By the way, did you notice Jesus' use of prophetic hyperbole here? The log in your eye—what a powerful image!)

Do you struggle with the temptation to judge others? If you do, go ahead and write it down in the margin of this book so you might ask God's help in working through this issue.

I'll leave it to you to read the rest of Matthew 7, but I'd like to lift up two things for you to consider as you do. The first is in verse 12. The verse begins with *so* (or *therefore*), meaning that this verse applies to everything Jesus had said up to that point and not simply the previous paragraph.[11] It is as if Jesus were saying, "So, in light of everything I've said up to this time, and by way of summarizing what I'm trying to teach you about how we treat each other in the Kingdom...." Then Jesus continued with verse 12: "In everything do to others as you would have them do to you; for this is the law and the prophets" (NRSV).

This is a vision of God's kingdom, and while Jesus wasn't the first to formulate it, he was the first we know of to turn it into a positive statement. Others had taught, "Refrain from doing to others what you don't want done to you." But Jesus went beyond that. The Kingdom is not simply about refraining from doing evil; it is about actively blessing others—it's about being salt and light for the world!

The second thing I'd like you to consider is the ending of Matthew 7, which is also the end of the Sermon on the Mount:

> "Therefore everyone who hears these words of mine and puts them into practice is like a wise man who built his house on the rock. The rain came down, the streams rose, and the winds blew and beat against that house; yet

it did not fall, because it had its foundation on the rock. But everyone who hears these words of mine and does not put them into practice is like a foolish man who built his house on sand. The rain came down, the streams rose, and the winds blew and beat against that house, and it fell with a great crash." (Matthew 7:24-27 NIV)

Several years ago, LaVon and I were looking at buying a rental property. We had a family member who needed a place to stay, and we thought that, with housing prices down, it might make sense to buy a house and rent it first to our relative, then later to others. We visited a house that on the multiple-listing sheet appeared to be an unbelievable deal. The house was just fifteen years old, and we knew that it would be perfect. But when we arrived, we were shocked to see the entire house tilting at an angle. The walls leaned, the doors and windows wouldn't open or close, and there were giant cracks in the sheetrock and in the basement walls and floors. It had a bad foundation built upon shifting soils. The agent said, "We call these homes 'dozer bait.' It's cheaper to bulldoze them down and start over than to fix them, because the houses were built on shifting ground."

How is your foundation?

The way Jesus lays out for us is not easy. We will fail at times and stand in need of his grace. But this way offers us a picture of what life is meant to look like in the kingdom of God. This ideal, though we fall short of it, beckons us to walk in the footsteps of Jesus and to grow into his likeness.

Reflection
Let Anyone with Ears Listen

"Listen! A sower went out to sow. And as he sowed, some seeds fell on the path, and the birds came and ate them up. Other seeds fell on rocky ground, where they did not have much soil, and they sprang up quickly, since they had no depth of soil. But when the sun rose, they were scorched; and since they had no root, they withered away. Other seeds fell among thorns, and the thorns grew up and choked them. Other seeds fell on good soil and brought forth grain, some a hundredfold, some sixty, some thirty. Let anyone with ears listen!" (Matthew 13:3-9 NRSV)

Parables are simple stories or metaphors in which some dimension of faith is explained by drawing upon analogies from everyday life. Jesus often spoke in parables and frequently used agricultural metaphors or stories.

In the Parable of the Sower, Jesus described four ways that people respond to the preaching and teaching of God's kingdom. The seed in the parable is the message of the Kingdom. The sower is Jesus and all who come after him in teaching, preaching, or sharing the message. The four soil types represent different ways that people respond to the message—that is, different conditions of the heart and, consequently, the impact of the Kingdom on the lives of various hearers and ultimately on the world.

The parable is an invitation to spiritual self-examination. We're meant to ask what type of soil we represent and to consider the "fruit" we bear in our lives. Is your soul like the hard path where the message of the Kingdom never really sinks in and takes hold? Is your soul like the rocky ground where the message of the Kingdom begins to take hold but the roots never go deep? When adversity strikes, do you quickly fall away from God's path? Perhaps your soul is like soil covered with thistles, so that the cares of the world and the desire for wealth choke out your quest for God's kingdom. The hope, of course, is that your heart is like the deep, rich soil that produces a harvest 30, 60, or 100 times over.

What does this last kind of heart look like? To me, it looks like Linda. Linda went to church her whole life, but she told me that for years her faith remained at a fairly superficial level. In her twenties, as a young mother, Linda cultivated a deeper relationship with Christ than she had known before. The message of the Kingdom really began to take root in her life.

Serving others became an increasingly important part of Linda's life. Most recently she has been volunteering eight to ten hours a week to coordinate our church's work with six urban core schools, most of whose students come from families living in poverty. She oversees ministries that deploy over 1,000 people from our church in everything from painting, to tutoring, to serving as pen pals, and to running book fairs. The work she makes possible has touched over 1,200 children and their families and may give them a fighting chance of rising out of poverty. The message of the Kingdom took root in her life, and it produced a 1,200-fold harvest.

Most of us will not see a harvest so dramatic, but we are each meant to bear fruit by living our faith so that others experience the reign of God. What kind of soil are you?

Lord, I want my heart to be like the rich, deep soil in the parable. I want my faith to grow deep and in turn to lead me to a life of love in action. Help me to do this, I pray. Amen.

From *The Way: 40 Days of Reflection*. Abingdon Press, 2012.

Travel Photos

Church of the Beatitudes, on a mountain above Capernaum

View from the Church of the Beatitudes

Interior, Church of the Beatitudes

Mediterranean Sea

Sidon

PHOENICIA

Tyre

MT. HERMON

ABILENE

Caesarea
Philippi

PANEAS

ITURAEA

ULATHA

TRACHONITIS

Lake Semechonitis

GALILEE

BATANAEA

MT. OF
BEATITUDES

Capernaum

GAULANITIS

AURANITIS

MT. ARBEL

Kursi

Sea of
Galilee

Sepphoris

Nazareth

MT. TABOR

DECAPOLIS

Caesarea

MT. CARMEL

MT. GERIZIM

Sychar

SAMARIA

PEREA

Joppa

MT. OF
TEMPTATION

Jericho

Baptism
at Jordan
River

JERUSALEM

Ein Karem

Qumran

Bethlehem

Herodium

JUDEA

Gaza

Lake Asphaltitis
(Dead Sea)

IDUMEA

N

A

B

A

T

A

E

A

N

A

B

**PALESTINE
AT THE TIME
OF JESUS**

N
W   E
S

SCALE OF MILES
0   5   10 15   20 25 30

4. Calming the Storm
The Sea of Galilee

On that day, when evening had come, he said to them, "Let us go across to the other side." And leaving the crowd behind, they took him with them in the boat, just as he was. Other boats were with him. A great windstorm arose, and the waves beat into the boat, so that the boat was already being swamped. But he was in the stern, asleep on the cushion; and they woke him up and said to him, "Teacher, do you not care that we are perishing?" He woke up and rebuked the wind, and said to the sea, "Peace! Be still!" Then the wind ceased, and there was a dead calm. He said to them, "Why are you afraid? Have you still no faith?" And they were filled with great awe and said to one another, "Who then is this, that even the wind and the sea obey him?"

Mark 4:35-41 NRSV

JESUS LOVED THE SEA OF GALILEE. It is mentioned in the Gospels more than forty times. Jesus gets in and out of boats nearly as many times. Many other times Jesus walks along the lakeshore. It isn't hard to imagine why this is. The Sea of Galilee is captivating.

Ask people who have been to the Holy Land to tell you their favorite part of the experience, and nine times out of ten they will tell you about taking a boat across the Sea of Galilee. Tour companies operate boats of varying sizes, made to look like ancient seafaring vessels. Leaving the port at Tiberias, you sail north and east and soon find yourself thinking, "I'm on a boat crossing the Sea of Galilee! Jesus and the disciples crossed this same water again and again! I'm sailing where Jesus sailed!" If you're like most people, you make your way to the front of the boat, blocking out all the people behind you, and you look at the lakeshore. There's been very little development on the Sea of Galilee. You're gazing upon the lake as it would have appeared to Jesus and his disciples.

Jesus' love of the lake resonates with me. Nearly all the books I've written were written, in part, at the Lake of the Ozarks, about two hours from my home. I sit on my friend's dock, Bible in hand, commentaries and books spread out over the table, and I read and pray while enjoying the beauty all around me. I feel that I can think more clearly and breathe more freely when I'm sitting at the lakeshore.

Some of the most beloved stories from Jesus' ministry occurred at the Sea of Galilee. In the rest of this chapter we're going to consider three of those stories: Jesus' calling of his first disciples, his calming the wind and waves, and the night when he came to his disciples walking on the water. As we study these three stories we'll consider how each of them answers the question, "Who is this man, Jesus?"

The Sea of Galilee

The Sea of Galilee is not a "sea" as most would think of one. It is a lake just seven or eight miles across and thirteen miles long—about 40,000 acres total. Today, as in biblical days, it is called by four names: Lake Kinneret or Lake Gennesaret (possibly from *kinnor,* the Hebrew word for harp, since the lake is shaped rather like a harp), Lake Tiberias, or the Sea of Galilee. At seven hundred feet below sea level, this is the lowest freshwater lake in the world. Its average depth is eighty-four feet, but in places it is one hundred and fifty feet deep.

Water from snowmelt on Mount Hermon, to the north, and numerous springs and tributaries all around the lake provide its water. The Jordan River flows in at the lake's northernmost point, flows out at its southernmost point, and forms an invisible line that divides the lake. Fisherman in biblical times spoke of "crossing over" the lake, which could mean simply moving from one side of the imaginary line to the other. For instance, Capernaum was to the west of where the Jordan enters the lake, and Bethsaida was to the east of the Jordan. The towns were just a few miles apart but when one sailed from Capernaum to Bethsaida one "crossed over" to the other side of the Sea.

Josephus, the first-century Jewish historian, records that in his day there were 230 fishing boats that worked the lake. Though fishing stock has been depleted in recent years, you can still eat "St. Peter's fish," caught fresh and grilled at several restaurants around the lake.

(Be prepared, though. They are typically grilled whole, including head, scales, fins, and eyes!) If you are looking for a chance to connect with the biblical story in your own town, simply go to the local store, buy a couple of tilapia, and cook them on the grill, for this is what St. Peter's fish are.

In the time of Jesus, Jews typically lived on the northwestern side of the lake, with Romans and Greeks to the south and east at Tiberias and Romans, Greeks, and other Gentiles on the eastern shore. The eastern side of the lake was a part of the "Decapolis"—the largely Roman and Greek region of the Ten Cities—and few Jews lived there. This is why, in the story of the man living among the tombs, a herd of swine was nearby. This story took place on the east side of the Sea of Galilee, where swine were raised. Jesus repeatedly crossed over to the Decapolis to minister in the region of the Gentiles.

Jesus Calls Fisherman to Be His Disciples
Luke 5:1-11

Each of the Gospel writers, in slightly different ways, tells the story of Jesus' calling his first disciples. Luke is a master at story telling, and the richness of details in his account makes it my favorite.

One morning Jesus was walking along the lakeshore near Capernaum, praying or thinking or just enjoying the morning. Someone spotted him and began to spread the word that Jesus of Nazareth was back in town. The townspeople had seen him work miracles, and they had heard him preach with genuine authority. Within a few moments a crowd had gathered around him, waiting for him to teach, or preach, or heal.

This is how it was with Jesus' ministry. He quickly became recognized wherever he went. And wherever he went there was a crowd of people, each of whom wanted a small piece of him. If he ever was wearied by it, he never showed it. Even when his disciples told him to send the crowds away, he refused. If there were people who might hear the Gospel, or those who needed help and healing, he was willing to stop what he was doing to touch them.

That particular morning, Jesus stopped and began to teach the people. But the crowd pressed in on him, anxious to hear what he had to say about God and the Kingdom. As they did, Jesus noticed two boats that had been pulled ashore. The fishermen were standing in the water, carefully cleaning their nets. Jesus stepped into one of the boats, which belonged to Simon Peter, and told him, "Simon, I need you and your boat. Would you push us out from the shore a bit? I'd like to teach the people." Simon did just that. He pushed the boat a few yards from the shore, dropped the anchor, and sat in the boat behind Jesus. As the boat gently rocked to and fro, Jesus taught the people about the Kingdom.

I love this first part of the story. Jesus imposed upon Peter and asked to borrow his boat. And so I ask you: If the Lord asked to borrow your boat, or your car, or something of value to you, would you lend it to him? Would you let Jesus borrow your "stuff"?

Last year one of our pastors was on her way to the airport with her husband Ben and their baby daughter Joy. At 4:45 a.m. it was still dark, and they were on a stretch of the highway where there were no streetlights. Suddenly two deer ran in front of their car. Ben missed one but hit the other, knocking out the headlights and sending them into a 180-degree spin, after which the car came to rest in the road. The engine died, and the family was pretty shaken up but okay. However, the car would not start and was not easily visible to traffic coming from behind.

Just then, a woman in a pickup truck pulled up behind them, turned on her flashers, and parked at an angle that would protect their car. The woman learned that Ben had been driving Molly and Joy to the airport and that there was still time for them to make their plane. Knowing that no cab company would pick them up in time, the woman said, "I can't leave you two here. Come on, get in my truck, and I'll take you to the airport." Ben stayed with the car awaiting the police, while Molly and little Joy were whisked away to the airport, some twenty-five minutes out of the way for the woman. When they arrived at the airport, Molly tried to pay the woman. She simply said, "I won't take your money. I was just trying to do something good."

I don't know if this woman was a Christian or not. What I do know is that in offering a ride to Molly and Joy, she became a modern Good Samaritan. As I see it, she let Jesus borrow her truck. Would you let Jesus borrow your stuff?

Now, the fishermen along the Sea of Galilee often fish at night. This was true in the first century, and it's true today. I've watched them going out in their small boats, two at a time, lighting flares to draw the fish to the surface and then pulling their nets behind them and hauling in the fish. (I asked one of the fisherman why he fishes at night, and he said the fish can see the nets during the day.) Peter had been fishing all night and, when Jesus stepped into his boat, was finally nearing the time when he could go home to sleep.

I wonder if Simon Peter's eyelids grew heavy as he sat behind Jesus, watching the crowds on the shore and listening to Jesus preach. Three years later he would succumb to sleep as the Master prayed in the Garden of Gethsemane.

Finally, Jesus turned to Peter and said, "Simon, put out into the deep water and let down your nets for a catch." I love this part of the story. Simon had blessed Jesus by allowing him to borrow the boat. Now Jesus wanted to bless Simon in return. But Luke records Peter's response: "Master, we've worked all night but have caught nothing." Luke doesn't mention a pause here, but I can hear it. With his words, Simon was protesting Jesus' request to help, hoping Jesus would say something like, "Hey, no problem, I know you're tired. Just take me back to shore, and we'll go fishing some other time." But Jesus remained silent.

Oh, the pregnant pause. What would Simon do? He was exhausted, disappointed, and perhaps a bit perturbed, and he had no idea that the direction of the rest of his life was hanging in the balance. Simon might have said, "Jesus, seriously, I'm really tired and I haven't slept. Can we do this another time?" If he had, I suspect Jesus would have agreed to turn back. But for some reason Simon didn't say that. Instead, he spoke words that would come to define his life, words that reflect the response of a disciple to the Lord: "*Because you say so,* I will let down the nets" (Luke 5:5 NIV, emphasis added).

Simon called to Andrew, "Bring the nets!" and off they went with Jesus, out a ways off shore, where they lowered their nets—in broad daylight, where the fish could see them—and within seconds there was a tremendous jerk on the back of the boat! Simon's eyes opened wide as he seized one end of the net, and Andrew pulled on the other. The haul of fish in the nets was unlike any he had ever seen, and certainly too many for him and Andrew to haul in alone. He stood in the boat and began waving to James and John to come and help.

When the excitement finally died down, after the catch was in the boats and everyone had a moment to stop and breathe, Peter looked at all those fish. You would expect a veteran fisherman to be beside himself with excitement and joy—he had just caught the biggest haul of fish he would ever see. You might think he would say, "Preacher, you've made my day, my month, my year! Thank you so much!"

Instead, Simon fell to his knees and said something completely unexpected: "Depart from me, for I am a sinful man, O Lord!" (Luke 5:8 ESV)

Simon had seen that Jesus was more than a carpenter and more than a teacher. Simon had seen something terrifying. In that boat, in that man, he had seen the power of God. He responded very much the same way Isaiah the prophet had responded to a vision of the heavenly throne room of God, when Isaiah cried out, "Woe is me...for I am a man of unclean lips and I live among a people of unclean lips" (Isaiah 6:5 NRSV). I think as Luke recounts this story, he intends for us to remember Isaiah.

Isaiah's story ends with the voice of the Lord speaking to the prophet and saying, "Whom shall I send, and who will go for us?" (6:8, NRSV) Notice what Jesus says to Simon in Luke 5:10: "Do not be afraid; from now on you will be catching people" (NRSV).

Peter would devote the rest of his life to serving the Master. He would be the prince of the Apostles and the rock upon which the church was built. He would travel the world proclaiming Christ. He would be imprisoned for Christ. And ultimately he would be crucified upside down in Jesus' name.

Peter's entire life hinged on a moment when, tired after staying up all night, he let Jesus borrow his boat and then heeded Christ's call to go out into the "deep waters" and let down his nets. Are you paying attention? These moments come into our lives when Christ needs to borrow our stuff or borrow us, when he nudges us to do what we don't feel like doing. When we do it simply because he says so, we find ourselves being used by him, and we experience life's greatest blessings and holiest moments.

Jesus Calms the Wind and the Waves
Mark 4:35-41

A second story on the lake is found in Mark 4 and repeated in Matthew 8 and Luke 8. In Matthew we learn that Jesus, after coming down from a mountain, had been in Capernaum all day with his disciples, preaching, healing the sick, and casting out demons. It was evening, and he was exhausted. He said to his disciples, "Let's get into the boat and go to the other side of the lake."

This was a little fishing boat, probably about twenty-seven feet long, and it would have held just a dozen people. This was the kind of boat Jesus and the disciples often used to cross the Sea of Galilee.

The disciples stepped into the boat and, as they began their two-hour journey across the lake, Jesus went to the back, lay down on a cushion, and fell asleep. After a while, a sudden and tremendous squall came up. The word used for this type of storm is *seismos*, a Greek word we translate as "tempest" or "earthquake." The wind was fierce, and rain poured down. Waves rocked the little boat, breaking over the sides until, as Mark says, "it was nearly swamped."

There they were, in a terrible storm at night, several miles from shore, in water 150 feet deep. Mark says, "The disciples woke him and said to him, 'Teacher, don't you care if we drown?'" (4:38 NIV)

I picture Jesus waking, looking at them, and smiling. He said, in effect, "You guys just don't get it, do you? I mean, weren't you with me when I cast out the demons? Didn't you watch when the lame man walked and the blind man suddenly could see? Do you really think this boat is going to sink while I'm asleep back here?"

The Jesus Boat

In 1986 there was a drought in the Holy Land, and the water level in the Sea of Galilee dropped precipitously, exposing the muddy lake bottom. An odd object was discovered protruding from the mud. When archaeologists studied it, they determined it to be a boat from the time of Jesus. The boat was excavated, carefully preserved, and placed in a museum for all to see. The image below shows what the boats of Jesus' day probably looked like. You can find out more about it and see images of the boat at www.jesusboat.com.

Mark says, "He got up. He rebuked the wind and said to the waves, 'Quiet, be still.' And the wind died down and it was completely calm" (4:39 NIV).

In that moment, Jesus demonstrated that he was Lord over the forces of the deep, and over the wind and the rain. The scene takes us back to that moment when Moses parted the waters of the Red Sea. Jesus had that kind of power over nature, and the disciples realized once again that they were not dealing with an ordinary man.

Notice that they called Jesus "Teacher." They had heard God speak through Jesus in such a way that they had set aside their lives and followed him. Still, they didn't yet know that he was more than a teacher, and their continuing doubt and fear prompted Jesus to say, "You of little faith, why are you so afraid?"

Even in the peace and calm after Jesus quieted the storm, Mark tells us, "They were terrified and asked each other, 'Who is this? Even the wind and the waves obey him!'" (4:41 NIV)

It was clear during the days of the Old Testament that there was only one who commanded the winds and the waves. Even modern-day meteorologists can do no more than predict storms; they can't stop them. But here the disciples encountered a man who spoke, and the winds and waves obeyed. We read in Psalm 89, "O LORD God Almighty, who is like you?... You rule over the surging sea; when its waves mount up, you still them" (8-9 NIV). When the disciples asked, "Who is this man?" they were beginning to realize that in some way they didn't yet understand, this man, this teacher and healer, brought God into their midst.

As Christians, we have struggled for two thousand years to express what the disciples sensed that day—that God had come to them in Jesus Christ. We use words such as *incarnation* and speak of Christ's deity. We do this because, throughout the Gospels and in our own day, we see that Jesus does the works of God, reveals the character of God, and in some mysterious way *is* God. Matthew captures the idea in the birth story of Jesus when he writes, "You shall call his name Immanuel, which means God is with us."

That day, Jesus brought peace in the midst of the storm. There is a lesson in this for today, since at times all of us will face a situation that terrifies us. It may be an illness that strikes us or someone dear to us. It could be divorce, an extended period of unemployment, or any number of other things. Individually and collectively, we will face strong winds and huge waves in the middle of night with no life jackets. In those moments, Jesus wants us to remember that if we invite him, he will always be in the boat with us.

That doesn't mean that we won't go through storms, or that we won't be terrified from time to time. Yet the story points to the truth that even in the midst of storms, he will be with us. We don't have to be afraid. He is the master even of death, so that the worst thing is never the last thing.

Bill is a United Methodist pastor and district superintendent who knows about the terrifying storms of life. He told me,

I was twenty-four years old and going to seminary to become a pastor. My wife and I had been married two years, and we had a six-month-old daughter. I was serving two tiny churches in Alabama part-time. That alone qualified as a storm! Then one day my wife said, "Honey, I don't feel very good. I think I need to go to the doctor."

We discovered she had a form of leukemia that doesn't respond well to treatment, and we spent the next two years in and out of the hospital. Just when it seemed that things were turning around, they would get worse again. I was completing my seminary degree while I spent much of my time in the hospital, tried to take care of our baby, and was afraid for what was happening with my wife. Finally the doctors said to us, "There's really no hope. She's not going to get better." We told the doctors that if there was anything they could do in terms of tests or experimental treatments, even if they didn't help her but might help somebody else after she was gone, then we were willing to go through them. And so for the last few months of her life the doctors used experimental treatments with my wife to learn what they could in order to help others.

She died after a two-year battle, right before Easter. I had graduated seminary, was serving as the solo pastor of a church, and was left as a single parent to care for our daughter. I had never felt a storm like that in my life. It was terrifying. Waves of fear and anger would crash against me and over me. Every day I wondered, How can I make it one more day? I can't do this. I just can't do this. And then I would hear Jesus speaking to me. Actually, I wouldn't just hear it. I would feel it in my body. I would feel him say, "Come on, get up. Today we can do this together. We really can." And I would take the next step and move forward into the next day. That was the storm when I felt Jesus in my boat, and he was the reason why I could get up every single day. I wish the storm had never come, but I have no doubt that his presence in my boat calmed the wind and waves and never let me drown.

If Jesus is not in your boat, what will you hold onto in the middle of the night, when the waves are seven or eight feet high and you don't have a life jacket? Jesus wants to be in the boat with you. It's a matter of faith. It's a matter of trust. We are meant to ask the question the disciples asked: "Who is this? Who is this man, that even the storms obey him?"

Jesus Walks on the Water
Matthew 14:22-33

Our third story also involves a storm. This time Jesus had been teaching all day in Bethsaida, also on the north shore of the Sea of Galilee but on the east side of the Jordan River. He had been casting out demons and healing the sick, and at sunset he said to his disciples, "Get in the boat and go on ahead to the other side. I'll see you there in the morning."

They asked how Jesus was going to get there, and he said, "Don't worry. I'll take care of that. Just go ahead." And then he went up to the mountain to pray all night. At three in the morning he could see the disciples out on the water, struggling, the winds blowing them as they strained against the oars, off-course in their attempt to cross the lake. And this time, without Jesus in the boat, they really were terrified.

Jesus decided to go to them, and he began walking across the water. The Gospel describes the incident in a rather casual way, as though Jesus were simply going to walk on by, checking as he passed to make sure they were all right.

But his presence put the disciples in a worse state. Already frightened to death of the storm and waves, they now saw what appeared to be a ghost out on the water. They cried out, and Jesus said, "Take courage. It is I. Don't be afraid" (Matthew 14:27 NIV).

In English, the phrase *It is I* is a bit awkward and doesn't give a true sense of what Jesus was saying. In Greek, it is *Ego eimi,* which means literally "I am." He was saying, "Take courage. I am. Don't be afraid."

Why would Jesus put it that way? It makes little sense until you remember a conversation God had with Moses by way of a burning bush. God said, "Moses, come near and take off your shoes. You're standing on holy ground." Moses took off his shoes, and God told him, "I have heard the cries of my people, who are slaves in Egypt. Now I want you to go to pharaoh in Egypt and tell him to let them go free." Moses stammered and said, essentially, "Do you think maybe you could find somebody else?" "No," God said. "I need you." Moses asked, "Well, who shall I tell them sent me?" (In essence he was saying, "What is the name of this God who is speaking to me from a burning bush?") God said simply, "My name is *I am* [or *I am that I am*]" (Exodus 3:5-14, paraphrase).

Now, thirteen hundred years later, Jesus stood on the water in the darkness, in the midst of a storm, telling these terrified men, "Be encouraged. I am. Don't be afraid."

You would think Simon Peter might urge Jesus to get in the boat and calm the waves, as Jesus had done before. Instead Peter said, "Well, if you are, then call me to come out on the water and walk with you." I can picture Jesus smiling and saying, "Come on" (Matthew 14:28, paraphrase).

It's a story we all know from Sunday school. Peter stepped out of the boat and began walking on the water, focused like a laser beam on Jesus, astounded at what he was doing.

Then a strong gust of wind came up, and instead of focusing on Jesus, Peter thought about the storm and the sheer impossibility of what he was doing, and for an instant he did the one thing he knew in his gut not to do. He looked down.

Dumped into the deep, he yelled, "Save me, Lord!" Jesus stretched out his hand, and Peter grabbed it. Jesus lifted him into the boat, then climbed in himself. The wind died down, and the disciples worshiped him, saying, "Truly you are the Son of God."

In this story, the disciples have reached a new understanding. They have gone from Simon Peter's statement "I'm a sinful man—please leave," to "Who is this man who calms the wind and the waves?" to this place, where the disciples have seen him walk on water and declare him to be the Son of God.

Psalm 77:19 tells us, "Your way was through the sea, your path, through the mighty waters" (NRSV). In Job 9:8, Job says, "[God] treads on the waves of the sea" (NRSV). Throughout the Hebrew Scriptures, only God did these things. And so Peter and the other disciples concluded that somehow, in a way they still could not fully explain, the one in their boat was "truly" the Son of God (Matthew 14:33 NIV).

The way this plays out practically was made clear to me recently when one of our church's staff members faced a double mastectomy. The day before her surgery she told me:

> Throughout this whole cancer experience, the visual I've attached to it is of Jesus calming the storm. Jesus has been a presence in my boat through all the loving people he's put around me. They remind me that he is here with me and that the waters can be calm. Today my whole team gathered in the hall at the church, wrapped me in a prayer shawl, and prayed for me. Our team and lots of other people—church members, friends, family—have continually written notes and e-mails, or they've called or stopped by for a hug. For me they are the boat and the hands and face of Jesus.

She said,

> I've learned so much about God's love as the recipient of all of this. Knowing that these people are praying

for me, feeling Christ's presence and love through them, has been the only thing that makes me calm and brings me peace. I know it will continue to do so tomorrow. It's like riding a wave of prayer. I can physically feel it, the way you do in a boat when the water is calm.

Who is in the boat with you? If you'll let him, Jesus will climb in and give you a "peace that passes all understanding." Trust that he is with you, that he cares for you, and that he still commands the wind and the waves, treads on the water, and has power even over death.

A century and a half ago, the words of a hymn written for sailors in the British fleet captured some of the power and peace we find in this story. It's usually referred to as the "Navy Hymn," and it has become a favorite of sailors and fishermen:

Eternal Father, Strong to save,
Whose arm hath bound the restless wave,
Who bid'st the mighty Ocean deep
Its own appointed limits keep;
O hear us when we cry to thee,
for those in peril on the sea.

O Christ! Whose voice the waters heard
And hushed their raging at Thy word,
Who walked'st on the foaming deep,
and calm amidst its rage didst sleep;
Oh hear us when we cry to Thee
For those in peril on the sea!

Most Holy Spirit! Who didst brood
Upon the chaos dark and rude,

And bid its angry tumult cease,
And give, for wild confusion, peace;
Oh, hear us when we cry to Thee
For those in peril on the sea![12]

We've all been at peril on the seas of our lives. Jesus still gives us peace when the storms rage.

Perhaps this is why architects refer to the central part of a church's sanctuary as the "nave." The word comes from the Latin *navis,* which means "ship." Every week, the church members gather as shipmates, with Christ as the captain, calming the wind and waves. When the service is over he sends us back upon the land of our daily lives to walk in the way, and to do his work. As we do we remember he promised "I am with you always, to the end of the age" (Matthew 28:20 NRSV).

Reflection
Fishing for People

As Jesus passed along the Sea of Galilee, he saw <u>Simon</u> and his brother <u>Andrew</u> casting a net into the sea—for they were fishermen. And Jesus said to them, "<u>Follow me and I will make you fish for people</u>." And immediately they left their nets and followed him. As he went a little farther, he saw <u>James</u> son of <u>Zebedee</u> and his brother <u>John</u>, who were in their boat mending the nets. Immediately he called them; and they left their father <u>Zebedee</u> in the boat with the hired men, and followed him. (Mark 1:16-20 NRSV)

I recently spent time with Yaeri, a Jewish fisherman who makes his living on the Sea of Galilee. I wondered what I might learn from this fisherman about the kind of people Jesus chose as his companions.

Yaeri was salt of the earth. I asked him what he loved about his work as a fisherman on the Sea of Galilee. He told me he loved the sea: "Every day is different. It is beautiful." Indeed, anyone who has been to the Sea of Galilee can testify to its beauty, as well as to how different it looks at various times of day and during changes in weather patterns. Those who have been to the Holy Land nearly always report that one of their favorite experiences was taking a boat across the Sea of Galilee, and most tours arrange for this.

I asked Yaeri, "Why do you think Jesus chose fishermen on this lake to be his first disciples?" His answer: "Fisherman make good friends. They are trustworthy and hard working."

Acts 4:13 notes of Simon Peter and John that "they were uneducated and ordinary men." The word *ordinary* here is the Greek word *idiotai*—a word that, at the time, signified untrained, unpolished in speech, or unskilled.

Jesus' first disciples were not the valedictorians of their seminary class. They were not those voted "most likely to succeed" in their high school class. They were men who likely did not finish school. They probably wouldn't have been anyone's first choice to lead a movement that would change the world.

When I think of them, I am reminded of a retired pastor I know. He struggled with stuttering his entire life. He was teased and harassed as a boy. But as a young man he heard God calling him to fish for people by becoming a preacher. This seemed to be an impossible calling; nevertheless he said, "Here I am, Lord." He went to school and ultimately became a Pentecostal preacher. He continued to stutter his entire life, but an interesting thing happened to him when he would stand in the pulpit to preach: his stuttering went away, and instead he delivered, with power and eloquence, the message of Christ. Ultimately God used him to build a church with many thousands of people in a low-income community. The church included former prostitutes and drug dealers worshiping side-by-side with business leaders and educators. It was one of the city's most diverse and dynamic congregations.

God seems to delight in using the *idiotai*—the ordinary, common, nothing-special kind of folks. Paul writes, "God chose what is foolish in the world to shame the wise ... so that no one might boast in the presence of God" (1 Corinthians 1:27, 29). Jesus comes to all of us who claim to be his disciples, calling us to follow him and he'll make us fishers of people. Are you willing to say yes?

Lord, help me to follow you faithfully, to be willing to lay down my net and join in your mission of fishing for people. Amen.

———————————————

From *The Way: 40 Days of Reflection*. Abingdon Press, 2012.

Travel Photos

Sea of Galilee from Valley of Doves

Sea of Galilee with boat

Sea of Galilee

Sea of Galilee

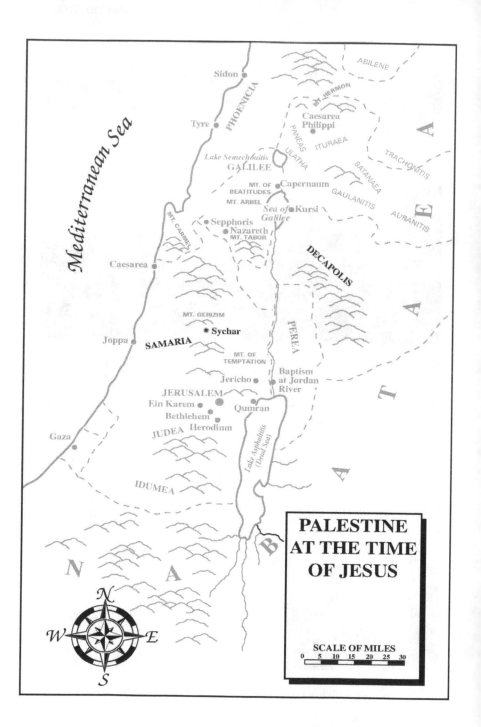

Sidon

Tyre

PHOENICIA

ABILENE

MT. HERMON

Caesarea
Philippi

PANEAS

ITURAEA

ULATHA

TRACHONITIS

BATANAEA

Lake Semechonitis

GALILEE

MT. OF
BEATITUDES

Capernaum

GAULANITIS

AURANITIS

MT. ARBEL

Sea of
Galilee

Kursi

Sepphoris

Nazareth

MT. CARMEL

MT. TABOR

Caesarea

DECAPOLIS

Mediterranean Sea

MT. GERIZIM

Sychar

PEREA

Joppa

SAMARIA

MT. OF
TEMPTATION

Jericho

Baptism
at Jordan
River

JERUSALEM

Ein Karem

Qumran

Bethlehem

Herodium

Gaza

JUDEA

Lake Asphaltitis
(Dead Sea)

IDUMEA

N

A

B

A

T

A

E

A

**PALESTINE
AT THE TIME
OF JESUS**

N
W · E
S

SCALE OF MILES

0   5   10   15   20   25   30

5. Sinners, Outcasts, and the Poor

Samaria

[Jesus] left Judea and started back to Galilee. But he had to go through Samaria. So he came to a Samaritan city called Sychar, near the plot of ground that Jacob had given to his son Joseph. Jacob's well was there, and Jesus, tired out by his journey, was sitting by the well. It was about noon. A Samaritan woman came to draw water, and Jesus said to her, "Give me a drink." (His disciples had gone to the city to buy food.) The Samaritan woman said to him, "How is it that you, a Jew, ask a drink of me, a woman of Samaria?" (Jews do not share things in common with Samaritans.) Jesus answered her, "If you knew the gift of God, and who it is that is saying to you, 'Give me a drink,' you would have asked him, and he would have given you living water."

John 4:3-10 NRSV

I'M NOT A COUNTRY MUSIC FAN, but there are a few country songs I really enjoy. Perhaps my favorite is Garth Brooks' hit "Friends in Low Places," in which Garth sings about showing up in cowboy boots at a black-tie affair to say farewell to the woman who broke his heart. She wants to be a part of high society. He's a cowboy. The refrain of the song begins with the cowboy proudly singing, "'I've got friends in low places." Every time I hear that song, I think of Jesus.

Jesus broke bread with the rich and poor alike. He ate with the "righteous" and the "sinners." But often the righteous were offended by him, while the sinners were drawn to him in droves. Jesus noted what was said about him by the religious leaders in Matthew 11:19: "Look, a glutton and a drunkard, a friend of tax collectors and sinners!" (NRSV).

In this chapter we're going to consider Jesus' "friends in low places," and what they tell us about him, and what it means to be his followers.

Let's begin with the Hebrew phrase *am ha-aretz*, often used in Jesus' time to indicate outsiders of one kind or another. It literally means "people of the land," and it had its origins in the days after the Israelites conquered Canaan. It referred to the Philistines and other Canaanites still present once the Israelites had settled the land. A derogatory term, it made it clear that these were not people to whom the land was promised, in essence saying, "They are less than we are." By the time of Jesus, the phrase meant foreigners as well as the unintelligent or unschooled, people seen as uncouth, unclean, or otherwise second-class in some way. It included the nonreligious and nominally religious—those who did not adhere strictly to the Law. If you were a faithful, religious Jew, "people of the land" were beneath you. To associate with them meant lowering yourself.

And yet these were the very people with whom Jesus spent a great deal of time. He healed their sick and fed their hungry. He was constantly roaming in their midst, touching the untouchable. He was interested in the very people others put down, the "lower classes" made to feel small in their society and culture.

As we walk in Jesus' footsteps, we will look at three categories of "people of the land": sinners, outcasts, and the poor.

Jesus' Affinity for Sinners

Not long after Jesus called Peter and Andrew, James and John, he stopped at the tax-collecting booth of a man who, like Simon Peter, was called by two names, Levi and Matthew. Matthew was stationed on a Roman road, collecting levies on goods such as fish being transported from Capernaum for sale elsewhere. He was a Jew from Capernaum who had bid on the right to hold the tax concession for that spot. He paid Rome in advance, then collected from those who came through. As you might guess, it was a system that invited abuse and extortion, since all the money he made over and above what he had paid the Romans was his. The fact that tax collectors worked for the Romans was, by itself, enough to make them traitors in the eyes of their own people. They were not welcome in synagogues, and upstanding Jews would not associate with them.

But Jesus walked up to him and said, "Matthew, I want you to follow me." Just as surprisingly, Matthew looked at Jesus and said yes. Here was a man who probably was making a great deal of money, and he simply shut down the tax concession for which he'd already paid the year's fee and set off to follow Jesus.

It's obvious there's quite a backstory here, but we're not privy to it. What could have made such a man decide to say yes to this wandering preacher and healer? Perhaps in spite of the money he had made, Matthew felt empty inside. Perhaps he had been feeling guilty about what he did for a living. He may have been longing for a new and better life and felt Jesus offered the chance for one. Or maybe Jesus' gaze so penetrated his soul that Matthew was unable to say no.

Whatever the reason, this was a huge decision—for both of them. It was a staggering, unbelievable pairing. In looking for a present-day analogy, I thought about the Kansas City area, where I live. It would be as if I went to a businessman who owned four or five of the city's strip clubs and said, "I can tell you're really good with business. You've got great customer-service skills, and so I'd like you to come be associate pastor at Church of the Resurrection."

I can imagine introducing him to our congregation, saying, "I'd like you to meet our new associate pastor. He's successfully run strip clubs, so I know he's a gifted leader and manager. He hasn't been to seminary, but I think he's really got potential." The congregants would think I'd lost my mind! But in this story we find Jesus doing a very similar thing. However, Jesus didn't see this tax collector as second-class. He saw something in Matthew that no one else was able to see.

That night, Matthew threw what Luke calls "a great banquet" for Jesus at his home, inviting all his friends, including many tax collectors. In the Middle East at that time (and still in many ways to this day), breaking bread with someone had major significance. It was the equivalent of saying, "I publicly proclaim you as someone I choose to associate with." The religious people of that day would not associate with the *am ha-aretz,* feeling that there was too much of a gap separating them. Even hygiene played a role, as there was an unwillingness to eat food prepared by someone who might not take cleanliness as seriously as a ritually observant Jew.

But Jesus ate with Matthew and his friends, talking and laughing and no doubt telling stories about a God who loves all his children. The guests must have been astounded that a Jewish rabbi was eating dinner with them, and the pious onlookers were of course shocked. Afterward, they said, "Why do you eat and drink with tax collectors and sinners?" It was a question Jesus would hear again and again.

In Luke 7, Jesus was invited to eat supper with a Pharisee, one of the righteous and respected members of society. The word *Pharisee* means "separated from" or "set apart," and members of the religious sect bearing that name separated themselves from the *am ha-aretz*, the less-thans, as part of an effort to be pure before God.

The host of this supper was a Pharisee named Simon. Those reclining around the U-shaped table would have included other important people from the town. As they were eating, there was a knock at the door. A woman whom the host knew to be a local prostitute walked in, looking for Jesus. When she saw him, she fell at his feet and began to weep.

Here again, there is a backstory we don't know. Did Jesus meet the woman earlier in the day? Maybe he looked at her as only he could, with eyes that said, "You are loved. You are somebody. You matter to God." Is it possible that for the first time since she was a girl, a man looking at her didn't just want her but cared about her and asserted that she had value as a person?

In any case, it's difficult to imagine how much nerve it took for a prostitute to show up at the house of this Pharisee, walk in, and in front of all those people approach Jesus the way she did. It's not difficult, however, to imagine how Simon the Pharisee and his guests responded. Questions must have swirled in their heads. What was Jesus' prior relationship with this woman? Why did he allow her to sit at his feet? What business did she have interrupting the supper?

Simon was outraged and no doubt embarrassed. He must have thought, *How dare she show up at my house and spoil my dinner party?* Luke records Simon's reaction upon seeing the woman touch Jesus: "If this man were a prophet, he would know who is touching him and what kind of woman she is—that she is a sinner" (Luke 7:39 NIV).

Hearing Simon, Jesus turned and told him a parable:

> "There were two men who each owed a certain moneylender money. One owed about two months' wages, the other nearly two years' wages. The moneylender canceled the debts of both. Which do you think was more grateful to the moneylender?" Simon rightly answered, "The one with the larger debt." Jesus continued, "That is correct. Simon, I need to ask you: Do you see this woman? I came to your home and you failed to offer me water to wash my feet, but she washed my feet with her tears. You did not greet me with the customary kiss, but she has not stopped kissing my feet. You did not offer me scented anointing oil, but she has brought perfume for my feet. Her sins were many but forgiven, and her response demonstrates her gratitude." (Luke 7:41-47, paraphrase)

Somehow the line *Do you see this woman?* always stands out to me. Simon indeed had seen her. She was an *am ha-aretz*, a prostitute. Jesus had seen her too, but as a human being, a child of God, a person of worth who was dearly loved and whose life had been marked by pain and shame.

The story leads me to ask myself, and to ask you, how do you see the *am ha-aretz* of our day? Do you see them as children of God, dearly loved, or do you see them as society sees them—sinners, outcasts, unclean?

Time after time, Luke's Gospel shows Jesus spending time with outcasts, breaking bread with sinners. By Luke 15, those watching him had had plenty of opportunities to be outraged: "Now all the tax collectors and sinners were coming near to listen to him. And the Pharisees and the scribes were grumbling and saying, 'This fellow welcomes sinners and eats with them'" (15:1 NRSV).

Religious people sometimes say things such as "God loves sinners but hates their sin." But when you're one of the sinners, that phrase sounds different than it sounds to the "righteous" people who say it.

Sin means straying from God's path, from the way that leads to life and joy and peace. That path is what we were created for. Straying from it leads us away from God, and often to pain.

There are times when *hate* may be an appropriate word to describe God's response to our sin. When our straying leads us to harm others, or to refrain from helping those who need us, or to be indifferent to their suffering, we might speak of God hating our sin. In the Gospels, the only time we find Jesus angry toward sin is when religious people act in self-righteous ways or when they fail to respond to those in need.

The longer we are Christians, the greater the temptation to become like the Pharisees. Over the years since I became a Christ follower at the age of fourteen, I've largely set aside some of the more obvious sins. But the sins I most often struggle with today are actually more dangerous than those earlier sins. They are more subtle and have to do with matters of the heart.

We used to have ash trees in our yard, and there were little worms called ash bores that tunneled their way into those trees and ate them from the inside out. A tree would look perfectly healthy for the longest time, until one day a strong wind would blow and the tree would break in half and come crashing to the ground. I think that's what Jesus was seeing in some of the religious leaders who separated themselves from "sinners" and so freely judged them. They looked pious on the outside, but inside they were eaten up with the worst kind of sin.

God is like a loving parent who watches as his children walk away from the path he wants us on. He doesn't like to see his children sin because he knows that sin can hurt us and others and can rob us of the joy he wants us to have. He knows that sin can separate us from him, and he grieves over that separation. Still, he doesn't stop loving us. He doesn't tell us how much he hates us or how much he hates what we do. He keeps beckoning and wooing us, reminding us of his love.

When my daughters were in their late teenage years, each of them had a period when she stepped away from God and the church. I knew intellectually that it was part of growing up, of beginning to think for themselves and finding their own identity. I also knew that most people who leave their faith in their teens and twenties return in their thirties and forties. Still, it was painful for me.

I had poured my whole life into bringing people to Christ and helping them know his love. The single most important thing for me when our daughters were born was that they would know God's love in Jesus Christ, that they would walk in that love, and that it would define their lives. When they said, "I don't want it, and I don't believe it," it tore me up. During those years, I would tiptoe into their bedrooms when they were asleep and kneel at their bedsides. Sometimes I would put my hand on their heads, lightly, so they wouldn't wake up. I would pray, "Lord, please don't let this one get away. Please hold onto her and don't let her go."

As painful as that period was, I never would have said to them, "I don't love you anymore" or "I can't eat with you anymore" or

"I think less of you now." Instead I tried to tell them, "I love you, and there is nothing you could do that would make me stop loving you. I'm disappointed that you are choosing to walk away from God, but I still love you and so does God."

That's the picture of God that Jesus was showing his disciples when he ate with sinners and tax collectors. He was saying, *This is what God is like,* as surely as when he related the parable of the prodigal son, or of the one sheep that wandered off, or of the lost coin. Jesus was living those parables.

I have a good friend who is a United Methodist pastor. His father, a fireman, died when my friend was ten or twelve. He told me, "My dad died without knowing Christ, and once I became a pastor I was determined to reach out to men and help them know Christ."

So he became a volunteer firefighter in every town where he served. He said, "My hope was to build friendships with these guys in the fire departments. I wanted them to know the love of God. I wanted to show that to them." He told me that, over the years, he had the joy of leading forty-six firefighters to Christ.

Many of us find that the longer we're Christians, the more likely it is that all our friends are Christian. Walking in the footsteps of Jesus, though, means building relationships intentionally with people outside the church. We do that to show them the love of Christ, whether they ever come to faith in him or not. In the process, at some point we may have the chance to say, "Would you like to come to church with me?" Sometimes when a friend is in need it's as simple as saying, "I'm praying for you each morning." At some point, you'll find yourself in a position to share the story of your faith and the difference Christ has made in your life.

Are you intentionally building relationships with the kinds of people Jesus befriended? Are you connecting with people outside the church? Are you allowing them to see the love of God shining through you? That's what Jesus did. At a time when most people saw God in terms of wrath and judgment, Jesus clearly painted a picture of God as a shepherd searching for his lost sheep, a father yearning for his lost children. Jesus went to the outsiders, befriended them, and sought to draw them to God, not by judgment but by love.

Outcasts

The second group of *am ha-aretz* was made up of outcasts, and there were two types we'll look at here. The first type of outcasts were the physically unclean, such as lepers. In biblical times, leprosy wasn't quite the same as Hansen's Disease, which is what modern-day leprosy is called. Biblical leprosy referred rather to a variety of skin disorders, including eczema, psoriasis, ringworm, and other conditions that caused open sores. These conditions were thought to be infectious, and the Law of Moses commanded that if you were diagnosed with one of them, you had to leave your home and your family and move outside of town. You were to keep your distance from others lest you infect them. If you saw someone approaching, you had to put your cloak up over your mouth and announce, "Unclean! Unclean! Don't come any closer!"

Can you imagine what it would feel like to be a person whom others could not hug or hold or even touch, who had to live outside the city gates until you were declared clean by a priest, something that might never happen?

For all the fear they generated, lepers were welcomed by Jesus. In Luke 5, a leper came and fell at Jesus' feet. He said, "Lord, if you are willing, you could make me clean" (5:12 NIV).

I love Jesus' reaction. He reached out and touched the man—sores and all—and said, "I am willing; be clean" (5:13 NIV). This was a step well beyond dining with sinners. Touching a leper was simply not done. And yet Jesus did it.

We need to ask: Who are the modern-day untouchables? Who are the lepers in our society, and what would it mean for us to touch them? More importantly, are there any untouchables in your life?

A few years ago, a group of us visited the Come Back Mission in a very poor section of the black township of Soweto, outside Johannesburg in South Africa. One of the mission centers was in a small town called Heavenly Village—an interesting name for a place that, for some, was a hell on earth. The residents were people who had been forcibly relocated under apartheid decades ago. They lived in shacks. Running water came from spigots in the middle of the dirt roads. There were dozens of children, and nearly half had HIV. Many of the women were dying of AIDS. We asked a mission worker how we could be of help, and she said, "I'd like you to visit the homes where many of the mothers are dying of AIDS."

The shacks were dark inside, with blankets over the windows. We would go inside and find a woman lying in bed, in the last stages of the illness. I knew I couldn't contract AIDS from touching another human being, but there was a hesitancy in my heart, something that repelled me and kept me from holding these women in my arms. I worked to overcome it and finally was able to sit on the edge of their beds and gather them into my arms or take their hands in mine and pray with them.

Who goes into such places to take the hands of the sick and dying and to love them? I think it is Christ-followers who seek to walk in the footsteps of Jesus. And while I had to work up the courage to do this, the folks at the mission have made this a daily part of their care for the dying there.

One of my heroes is Nancy Brown. I've been her pastor for twenty years. Nancy has made numerous trips to Africa to look for ways of helping women and men who live in debilitating poverty and have been affected by HIV. She described one trip to a rural village in South Africa, where children swarmed around her and wanted her to hold them. Picking up one little boy, she noticed little worms coming out from under the skin of his feet. Most of us would recoil from that sight, but Nancy just held the child in her arms. She was the presence of Christ for him, and in that moment she was walking in the footsteps of Jesus. I hope to be more like Nancy when I grow up.

A second type of outcasts in the time of Jesus were people considered unclean for other reasons. They may have been of the wrong religion. They may have had an emotional malady. Among the largest of these groups in Jesus' time were the Samaritans. They were despised to the point where Jews traveling from the Galilee region in the north to Jerusalem or Judea in the south would go hours or days out of their way to avoid passing through the region of Samaria that separated the two.

The bad blood between the Samaritans and Jews went back eight centuries before Christ, to a time when the Assyrian Empire conquered Israel and forcibly removed most of its citizens. (You can read about it in 2 Kings 17.) The Assyrians then relocated other conquered peoples to the land of Israel to take the place of the exiled Israelites. Some Israelites remained in the land, and they intermarried with these transplants. Their offspring were known as Samaritans.

Samaritans were seen as "half-breeds" by the Jews, even though the Samaritans adopted many beliefs and practices of the Jewish faith. Nevertheless, Samaritans were not allowed to worship at the Temple in Jerusalem, so they built their own temple on Mount Gerizim in Samaria. The Samaritans considered

Samaria

The region of Samaria was in the center of the Promised Land. (See the map at the beginning of this chapter.)
Today the West Bank is roughly this same region. Most
tour groups that come from America and travel from the
Galilee in the north to Jerusalem in the south tend to
do as ancient Jews did: bypass the West Bank, or the
ancient region of Samaria. Why do they do this? Often
it's because Americans believe that passing through the
Palestinian-controlled area of the West Bank is unsafe.

Much is missed by avoiding the West Bank, as it is a
beautiful part of the country. Going south from Galilee,
travelers pass first through the lush Jezreel Valley, the
region's breadbasket, where hundreds of thousands of
olive trees grow and tens of thousands of acres are cultivated in other crops. The ancient town of Megiddo is
located here (though on the Israeli side of the valley). In
the book of Revelation, the Jezreel Valley is the Valley of
Armageddon, where the final battle between the forces
of good and evil will take place. It is appropriate that
John, the author of Revelation, placed the battle here,
as over the years the Jezreel Valley has been the site of
many major battles.

Continuing to the south, the land begins to rise, slowly
at first and then quite dramatically, as the hill country and
Samaritan mountains rise from the plain. If you visit this
area, you'll want to see the ruins atop Mount Samaria,
including the town of Samaria, also known during the
New Testament period as Sebaste, where you will find

the remains of a temple to Augustus, an amphitheatre, and what some believe was an ivory palace belonging to King Ahab and Queen Jezebel. Near the palace is what is left of a church, where a small underground chapel is said to mark the burial place of John the Baptist. Standing atop this mountain, you'll find the scenery below to be lush, green, and beautiful. Wildflowers, olive groves, shepherds tending their sheep, and acres of crops can be viewed in the valleys below. It is easy to see why the kings of ancient Israel built their palaces here.

Not far away, to the south and east, the modern Palestinian town of Nablus was built atop the ancient village of Shechem (known during the New Testament period as Sychar). The village was built along the mountainsides and into the valleys. Towering above the site of Sychar is Mt. Gerazim, the mountain that Samaritans considered sacred, where they built their temple. Ascending Mount Gerazim, you can walk among the ruins of the ancient temple as well as the remains of a Byzantine-era church. Here, in the modern-day village adjacent to the ruins, you'll come across one of the final remaining communities of Samaritans. A history museum will tell you their story. You can also walk in the area where Samaritans still offer the Passover sacrifice each year.

From the ruins of the church atop Mount Gerazim, you can see the red roof of the St. Photina Orthodox Church and monastery. In the Orthodox tradition, St. Photina is the name given to the woman Jesus met at Jacob's Well, a woman who was part of the *am ha-aretz*.

When I travel to the Holy Land, this beautiful twentieth-century church is always a highlight for me. On each side of its altar are stairs that lead down to Jacob's well. There is no reason to doubt that this well was in fact the very place where Jesus asked a Samaritan woman to give him a drink (the story from John 4 that appears at the beginning of this chapter). Today, visitors can still draw water from the well and drink it. If you do, you may find that for a moment you're there with Jesus and the woman, drinking from the well they drank from.

If you watch the video that is available with this book, I'll take you to the well, then introduce you to a Samaritan priest, one of only 750 Samaritans still living.

(and still consider) themselves the true Israelites, while the Jews viewed the Samaritans as heretical, unclean *am ha-aretz.*

In the text at the beginning of this chapter, we find Jesus traveling from Judah to Galilee, and John tells us that Jesus "had to go through Samaria." In actuality, as explained above, no one *had* to go through Samaria. Jews could and frequently did go out of their way to avoid Samaria. Jesus chose to travel through Samaria because he cared about the Samaritan people. It was just one more of the many surprising things Jesus did.

As Jesus passed through the region, he came to the town of Sychar, not far from Mount Gerazim, the holy mountain. Arriving at midday, he sent his disciples into the town for food and waited outside, sitting near the town's water source, Jacob's Well. He knew there was a woman who would come to fetch water. Women typically did this in the morning and shared fellowship around the well, so a woman who came at midday would have been unusual—either because she chose not to associate with the other women or because she was not welcome among them. I believe this woman was considered an *am ha-aretz* by the people of her own Samaritan village—people who themselves were considered *am ha-aretz* by the Jews. She was, then, the lowest of the low. John tells us that she had been married and divorced five times, and in that society divorce would have come with quite a stigma. Further, she was now living with a man who was not her husband.

When the woman arrived at the well, Jesus said to her, "Give me a drink."

"Really?" she replied. "You're a Jew, a rabbi, and you want a drink from me?" John reminds us parenthetically that Jews did not share things in common with Samaritans, particularly when it came to eating and drinking. This was every bit the social divide that existed in the American South in the 1960s and before, when there were two bathrooms and two drinking fountains, one each for blacks and whites. And yet Jesus was going to drink from her cup.

"If only you knew whom you were talking to," said Jesus, "you would ask of me and I would give you living water and you would never thirst again."

Think of it. Jesus sought out a woman who was considered an outcast even among the Samaritans. She had found only rejection from the men she had loved. And yet Jesus offered her life—living water—and a love that would satisfy the longings of her heart. It is interesting to note that this woman became, in John's Gospel, the first person to whom Jesus openly revealed himself to be the Messiah. The story ends with the woman returning to the town and telling others that she had met the Messiah. John records, "Many Samaritans from that city believed in him because of the woman's testimony." In other words, a woman who had been divorced five times and was living with another man became the first missionary to the Samaritans.

One final word about this incident. The backdrop for the story is found in Genesis 29 (and perhaps also Genesis 24), where Jacob went to a well and met Rachel, a lovely virgin who became his wife. Jesus, though he wasn't choosing a wife, went to a well said to belong to Jacob and there offered living water to a scandalous woman who had been married and divorced multiple times. Jesus never married, but had he married I have the distinct impression that he would have chosen a woman whom others would have considered scandalous or unclean or worthless.

The Poor

The third group of *am ha-aretz* Jesus associated with were the poor. Though the Hebrew faith called for compassion and mercy toward the poor, giving them charity and actually caring for them were two different things. Many looked at the poor the way some do today, saying, "They're lazy, and they make bad choices. I'll help a bit, but that's it."

Jesus' own concern for the poor was evident from the beginning. His ministry began with them. Luke tells us that in Jesus' very first sermon in his home town of Nazareth, the text that he chose was from Isaiah: "The Spirit of the Lord is upon me, because he has anointed me to bring good news to the poor" (Luke 4:18 NRSV).

Jesus routinely fed, healed, and ministered to the poor. When he ministered to the rich, he called them to compassion and concern for the poor and those in need. It was not a suggestion. It was not optional. It was part of life in the Kingdom.

Three of Jesus' most famous parables were meant to help us understand how to look at and minister to the poor and those in need, whatever form that need might take. First was the parable of the Good Samaritan. The parable was scandalous when Jesus told it, both for the way he portrayed the religious leaders and for the fact that he made a Samaritan the hero of the story.

Jesus told the parable in response to a question from a teacher of the law: What must be done to inherit eternal life? Jesus asked for the man's thoughts on the question, and the man replied by quoting the two great commandments: "You shall love the Lord your God with all your heart, and with all your soul, and with all your strength, and with all your mind; and your neighbor as yourself." Jesus said to the man, "You have given the right answer; do this, and you will live." But the man probed further, asking, "Who is my neighbor?" (Luke 10:25-29 NRSV).

In essence the religious leader was asking, "Jesus, whom do I not have to love?" It was in response to that question that Jesus told the parable of the Good Samaritan.

Jesus said that a certain man was walking from Jerusalem to Jericho, about fifteen miles down a road that wound through the wilderness. On the way, the man was accosted by bandits, beaten, robbed, stripped naked, and left for dead. Two religious leaders passed by and saw the man, yet neither stopped to help.

Then along came the Samaritan. Seeing the injured man, he bandaged the man's wounds and put him on his own donkey, then paid for his food, clothing, shelter, and medical care.

"This," Jesus said, "is what it means to love your neighbor as yourself. This is how to be a neighbor."

Why didn't the religious leaders stop to help? Perhaps they were fearful of being attacked—maybe the whole thing was a trap. Perhaps they worried that if the man was dead, they would become ceremonially unclean by touching him and hence would be unable to fulfill the commitments they had made for the day.

Perhaps they were running late to Jericho and didn't feel they had the time to get involved.

In preaching on this text, Dr. Martin Luther King noted that the two religious leaders asked the question, "What will happen to me if I stop to help?" In contrast, the Samaritan asked the question, "What will happen to him if I don't stop to help?" Which question are you most likely to ask when you see someone in need?[13]

Jesus also told the parable of the Sheep and the Goats, in which he described the last judgment. "The Son of Man will return one day," he said. "He'll gather all the nations before him as a shepherd gathers the sheep and the goats, and then he'll separate them. He will send the goats away, but to the sheep he's going to say, 'Enter into my father's kingdom.'

"Here are the criteria that I will use to judge on that day: I was hungry and you gave something to eat. I was thirsty and you gave me something to drink. I was naked and you clothed me, a stranger and you welcomed me in, a prisoner and you visited me. And if you wonder when you did that, I will tell you that inasmuch as you've done these things to the least of these, you have done it to me" (Matthew 25:31-46, paraphrase).

This parable can be unnerving to people who have been taught that the only thing required for them to go to heaven is simply accepting Jesus as Lord and Savior. But in the Gospels Jesus says that not everyone who says to him, "Lord, Lord!" will enter the Kingdom. The true sign that we trust in Christ as Lord is that we follow him and seek to do his will. He saves us not merely so that we can go to heaven, but so that we can be instruments of his redemption, salvation, and compassion in the world. As James notes, "Faith without works is dead." Our faith is meant to manifest itself in a concern for the *am ha-aretz,* who are the poor and needy.

Finally, in Luke 16, Jesus told the parable of a rich man who lived in a fabulous home—think "gated community"—with the finest things to eat and drink. Outside the gate sat a poor leper named Lazarus who was too sick to work. Such was his sickness and poverty, said Jesus, that the dogs would come and lick his sores. Lazarus was hungry, and day after day he lay outside the gate, longing for someone in that affluent neighborhood to stop and offer him some something to eat, or help of any kind. Every day, the rich man simply stepped over him as he went about his business.

Eventually both men died, and Lazarus was taken to heaven, where he was comforted in the bosom of Abraham. The rich man, meanwhile, found himself in the flames of hell. The two could see each other across a great chasm, and the rich man cried out, "Father Abraham, please help me." But Abraham replied, "Remember, during your life you had plenty, and Lazarus had nothing, and you didn't care."

Jesus cared about the underdog, the mistreated, the down-trodden—the *am ha-aretz*. If we are going to be his disciples and walk in his footsteps, we must do the same. Christians have always understood that part of our work is to be the hands and feet of Christ in caring for the poor. Sometimes it begins with a handout, but we are meant to look for ways to offer a hand up. At the church I serve, we invest in ministries aimed at moving people to self-sufficiency. We invest in education. We work in the inner city. In our prison ministry, men from the congregation go regularly to Lansing and Leavenworth penitentiaries. It is a requirement for membership that every member will serve the poor or others in need somewhere outside the walls of the church every year, and those who are able are asked to partici-pate in a mission trip once every five years.

A remarkable thing happens as our members become engaged in ministries with the poor. They find their own lives enriched, their faith deepened, their sense of meaning and fulfillment in life transformed.

Jesus loved the outcasts. He abhorred religious people who made others feel small. In Luke 19:10, Jesus told the religious leaders that he came to "seek out and to save the lost" (NRSV). When I was a fourteen-year-old boy reading the Gospels for the first time, it was this compassion and love for the nobodies, the ne'er-do-wells, the poor and the outcasts, that drew me to Jesus. I loved this about Jesus then. I still love this about him today.

Jesus had friends in low places. Followers of Jesus befriend the *am ha-aretz,* the people of the land. They love sinners. They welcome the outcasts. They care for the poor. This is the way Jesus lived, and it's the way we live when we walk in his footsteps.

Reflection
The Women in Jesus' Ministry

> Soon afterwards he went on through cities and villages,
> proclaiming and bringing the good news of the kingdom of
> God. The twelve were with him, as well as some women who
> had been cured of evil spirits and infirmities: Mary, called
> Magdalene, from whom seven demons had gone out, and
> Joanna, the wife of Herod's steward Chuza, and Susanna, and
> many others, who provided for them out of their resources.
> (Luke 8:1-3 NRSV)

We typically think of Jesus traveling with his twelve disciples as he "went through the cities and villages proclaiming and bringing the good news of the kingdom of God" (Luke 8:1 NRSV), but Luke tells us that women traveled with him, too. So many of the Gospel stories involve Jesus' ministry with women. It is clear that he valued women, had compassion for them, saw them as beloved children of God, and, by his interest in them, demonstrated the value God places on women.

Jesus' attitudes toward women stood in contrast to the cultural and religious traditions of the period. Josephus, the first-century Jewish historian wrote: "The woman, says the Law, is in all things inferior to the man."* Women were treated as the property of their husbands and fathers. Yet Jesus treated women with value and respect.

Notice the kinds of women who were following Jesus. Luke tells us they had been cured of evil spirits and infirmities. What kind of infirmities had they suffered from?

The Gospels report that these included internal bleeding, fevers, and maladies then thought to be caused by demons, though now these are often associated with mental illness. We also know that Jesus offered grace to prostitutes, women caught in the act of adultery, and a woman divorced five times and living with a man who was not her husband. We also know that Jesus was concerned not only for Jewish women, but also for Samaritan and Gentile women as well.

The women Luke describes were more than followers. They provided support for Jesus and the twelve out of their own means. We learn in the Gospels that it was the women who stood at the foot of the cross while the male disciples, with the exception of John, were in hiding. It was the women who went to the tomb while the men continued to hide. And it was to Mary Magdalene that Jesus first appeared after the Resurrection. She became the first person to proclaim the resurrection of Christ.

I don't know where I would be without the female disciples who have entered my life. My grandmother was the first to share Christ with me. My mom took me to church. Two women encouraged me to consider being a pastor. My wife has been my partner in ministry, and most of the best ideas I ever had were really hers. In the church I serve, half of our leaders—lay, staff, and clergy— are women. Our aim for equality is not an effort at political correctness but at congregational effectiveness. Women made possible the ministry of Jesus in the first century, and they make his ministry possible today.

Lord, thank you for those women who have come into my life. Thank you for demonstrating the value of women in your ministry and, through them, teaching us how you value women today. Amen.

* From Flavius Josephus, *Against Apion* (trans. H. St. J. Thackeray; Loeb Classical Library; Cambridge, Mass.: Harvard University Press), 2. 200–201.

From *The Way: 40 Days of Reflection*. Abingdon Press, 2012.

Travel Photos

Ancient city of Samaria

Jacob's Well Church, in modern city of Nablus

Interior, Jacob's Well Church

Likely location of Jacob's Well, beneath church

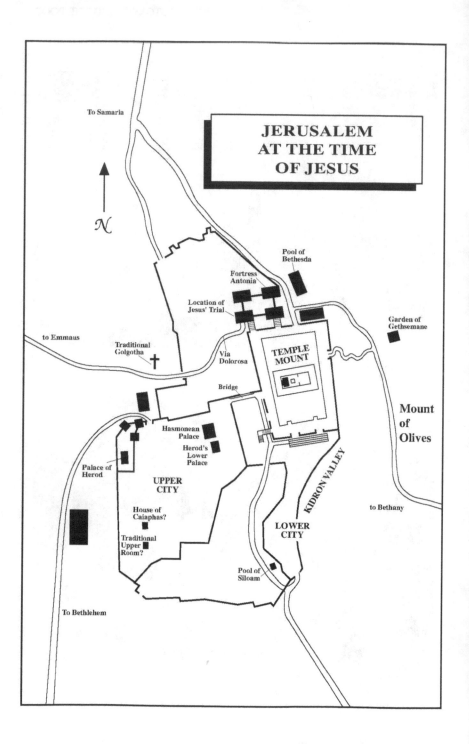

To Samaria

𝒩

JERUSALEM
AT THE TIME
OF JESUS

Pool of
Bethesda

Fortress
Antonia

Location of
Jesus' Trial

Garden of
Gethsemane

to Emmaus

Traditional
Golgotha

Via
Dolorosa

TEMPLE
MOUNT

Bridge

Mount
of
Olives

Hasmonean
Palace

Herod's
Lower
Palace

Palace of
Herod

UPPER
CITY

KIDRON VALLEY

to Bethany

House of
Caiaphas?

LOWER
CITY

Traditional
Upper
Room?

Pool of
Siloam

To Bethlehem

6. The Final Week
Jerusalem

Then they brought the colt to Jesus and threw their cloaks on it; and he sat on it. Many people spread their cloaks on the road, and others spread leafy branches that they had cut in the fields. Then those who went ahead and those who followed were shouting, "Hosanna! Blessed is the one who comes in the name of the Lord! Blessed is the coming kingdom of our ancestor David! Hosanna in the highest heaven!"

Mark 11:7-10 NRSV

THUS FAR WE HAVE WALKED IN THE footsteps of Jesus to the Jordan River near Jericho where he was baptized and to the wilderness of Judea where he was tempted. We journeyed with him to his home base of Capernaum where he healed the sick, walked with him up the mountains where he taught about the kingdom of God, sailed across the Sea of Galilee where he calmed the winds and the waves, and observed his ministry among friends in low places. We have not covered everything that Jesus said and did—this book is not meant to take the place of reading the Gospels—but I have sought to summarize the major themes, movements, and places in Jesus' three-year ministry, so that we might know who Jesus is and follow in his footsteps as modern-day disciples.

It is traditionally thought that Jesus' public ministry, from baptism to crucifixion, was a period of three years—156 weeks, or roughly 1,000 days. While the Gospel writers attempt to summarize this entire period for us, they clearly believe that the final week, the last seven days of Jesus' life, was the most important. We call this Holy Week, and Matthew devotes nearly 30 percent of his Gospel to this week and the events that followed it. Mark allocates nearly 40 percent of his Gospel to Holy Week. Though only 20 percent of Luke's Gospel is dedicated to the last week of Jesus' life, when we include Luke's account of Jesus' journey to Jerusalem leading up to the last week, 62 percent of the Gospel is focused here. And 47 percent of John's Gospel describes the events of Holy Week and beyond. Clearly the events of this final week are of utmost importance in the story of Jesus.

Jesus arrived in Jerusalem just as the week-long festival of Passover was about to begin. The city's population swelled as more than 200,000 visitors came to the Holy City for the celebration of Israel's defining story—how God had delivered the Israelites from slavery in Egypt.[14] Jesus and his disciples came to Jerusalem through Jericho, where Jesus had eaten with Zacchaeus the tax collector and opened the eyes of blind Bartimeus—two more friends in low places. John tells us that Jesus had eaten supper the evening before his "triumphal entry" into Jerusalem in the town of Bethany, on the back side of the Mount of Olives, at the home of Mary and Martha, where he stayed the night. Finally, on Sunday morning, Palm Sunday, Jesus entered Jerusalem for the Passover. Five days later he would be put to death.

During this, the final week of his life, Jesus would be hailed, however briefly, as a king. Yet the events that would follow made clear he was a very different kind of king than the crowds, and perhaps even his disciples, had hoped for. The crown he would wear was a crown of thorns. His enthronement would occur on a cross.

As we ponder the events of that week, we ask: What kind of King is Jesus?

Sunday:
Prince of Peace

On the morning we now celebrate as Palm Sunday, Jesus sent his disciples to the village atop the Mount of Olives to fetch a donkey that would be waiting for him. It was an odd errand, since throughout the Gospels there is no record of Jesus riding a donkey any other time. He always walked. In fact, he had just walked the ninety miles from Galilee to Jerusalem. So why, half a mile from the Temple, would he ask for a donkey?

Riding a donkey is a richly symbolic act, one that goes back to King David, the prototypical Jewish king. The royal animal David rode was not a steed but a donkey, which was more sure-footed than a horse on the rocky, hilly terrain of Palestine, and able to travel farther on less water. The donkey, moreover, was a humble beast reflecting David's identity as the shepherd king. Davidic kings from that time on rode donkeys or mules to identify with David.

Even more important for the Palm Sunday story is the prophet Zechariah's promise, given to the Jews five hundred years before the time of Christ: "Rejoice greatly, O daughter Zion! Shout aloud, O daughter Jerusalem! Lo, your king comes to you; triumphant and victorious is he, humble and riding on a donkey" (Zechariah 9:9 NRSV). Everyone in the crowd would have known these words and their promise of who would come riding on the donkey, so that when Jesus met up with his disciples and mounted the donkey, the people knew instantly what was happening. He was giving a clear signal that he was the long-awaited King promised by the prophets. Finally, Jesus was openly proclaiming he was the Messiah!

As Jesus rode down the Mount of Olives toward Jerusalem, the people began to wave palm branches, a sign of victory and celebration among Jews and Romans alike. They shouted "Hosanna!" (which means "Save us now!") and "Blessed is he who comes in the name of the Lord!" They were quoting Psalm 118:26 (NIV), which they would have known by heart since childhood as it was recited every year at the Feast of Tabernacles and during the Feast of Passover. The Psalm was written to welcome kings back to Jerusalem as they returned victorious from war. It was understood to refer as well to the Messiah who would come and deliver the people. The people were hailing Jesus as their King, and this was his royal procession.

The Romans understood the symbolism too, and that scared the Pharisees. They ran to Jesus and said, "Tell your disciples to keep it down. If the Romans hear this kind of talk, they'll kill us all." Jesus replied, "Listen, if the people weren't shouting

'Hosanna,' the very rocks and stones would have to shout these words." With waving palms, shouts of praise, and calls for deliverance in the air, Jesus, the son of a carpenter, entered Jerusalem in a royal procession, riding on a donkey.

There were two other royal processions entering Jerusalem that day. Pontius Pilate, the Roman governor of Judea, would have entered the city from the west, coming from Caesarea by the Sea and bringing with him at least 1,000 Roman soldiers on chariots, on horseback, and on foot, with all their weapons and regalia. The show of force was designed to suppress any thoughts of rebellion during the Passover. After all, the festival marked the Jews' release from bondage in Egypt, so the celebration always carried an undertone of hope for liberation—a hope that God was going to free his people again.

Pilate's procession was a show of force meant to remind the people of Jerusalem who was in control. For good measure, he intended to crucify several rebels on Thursday of that week, the day of preparation for Passover, so that as the Passover meal was celebrated, the Jews were reminded of Rome's power.

The other procession was that of King Herod Antipas, who entered from the north with his own retinue and royal soldiers. Antipas ruled over the Galilee and Perea, north and east of Judea, and he, like Pilate, knew how to use violence to suppress the people. It was he who had beheaded John the Baptist. Antipas was the son of King Herod the Great, and there were many who hoped that one day the Romans might give him rule over the entire land. His supporters lined the streets as he entered the Holy City, cheering as he arrived.

Two of the three rulers entering Jerusalem in parades on that Palm Sunday were iron-fisted men known for their cruelty. They were perfectly willing to kill in order to hold power, and they used impressive shows of force to demonstrate that fact.

Jerusalem

The walk down the Mount of Olives, retracing Jesus' steps on Palm Sunday, is dramatic and moving. From the top of the Mount of Olives visitors have a panoramic view of Jerusalem. From here you can see the location of nearly every event of Jesus' final week: the Temple Mount, the Upper Room, the Kidron Valley, the Garden of Gethsemane, the traditional location of Jesus' trial before Pilate, the Church of the Holy Sepulcher that was built atop Calvary where Christ was crucified, and the tomb where he was laid to rest.

If you visit, be prepared for the many people who will try to sell you postcards and olive wood crosses and even a man who, for a few dollars, will let you sit atop his camel for a picture.

The side of the Mount of Olives is covered in tombs. The adjacent Kidron Valley is also considered the Valley of Jehoshaphat—the biblical valley of the last judgment—and the symbolism of these tombs is powerful. Jews are buried with their feet toward the Temple Mount, so that when the Messiah returns the dead will stand, facing the Holy City, awaiting judgment. There are thought to be 150,000 people buried on the Mount of Olives. I imagine the bones rattling in their graves on that first Palm Sunday as Jesus the Messiah walked down the mountain.

As you descend the Mount of Olives down a narrow winding road, you'll come to a chapel, on your right, which marks the traditional location of Christ's weeping over the city. Pausing here, you can stop and read

the story in Luke 19:41-44. Then, making your way to
the base of the mountain, you can pause again to visit
the Garden of Gethsemane, with its ancient olive trees
thought to have been there when Jesus prayed in the
garden.

Among the highlights of a visit to Jerusalem is the
place that Christians and Jews call the Temple Mount.
(This designation is offensive to Muslims since, as they
will tell you, the Temple has not stood on this site for
2,000 years, whereas the Muslim Dome of the Rock
has been there for over 1,300 years. For Muslims this
place is called *Haram al Sharif,* the Noble Sanctuary.)
When visiting the Temple Mount, one recalls that Jesus
drove out the merchants and money changers here. He
taught in the Temple courts. It was here that he sealed
his death sentence by denouncing the religious leaders.

The most meaningful part of a visit to Jerusalem, in
my experience, is retracing the final hours of Jesus' life.
It is easiest to do this starting with Jesus' time of prayer
in the Garden of Gethsemane. Stand among the ancient
olive trees, and then enter the Church of All Nations,
also known as the Basilica of Christ's Agony, where the
art and architecture take you to that night when Christ
prayed, "Father, take this cup from me. Yet not my
will but thy will be done." Plan to spend at least thirty
minutes there exploring the art and praying at the rock
formation where tradition says Jesus prayed that night.

Next, imagine yourself walking across the Kidron
Valley with Jesus after his arrest. As you move through
the valley and then up the stairs on the other side, you'll

pass by the Temple walls and hike uphill until you come to the Church of St. Peter Galicantu, the traditional location of Jesus' trial before the Sanhedrin and Peter's three-fold denial of the Lord. A dungeon carved into the stone, perhaps once a cistern, allows visitors to imagine Jesus here, imprisoned, awaiting the morning hours when he would be taken to Pontius Pilate for a second trial. Read the account here of Jesus' trial before the council.

From Galicantu you can walk into the Old City of Jerusalem, through the bazaars, imagining Jesus being led by the guard in the ancient city and taken to Pontius Pilate at Pilate's palace or perhaps the Fortress Antonia. You can visit the first- or early second-century Roman roadway under the Sisters of Zion convent and picture the place where Jesus was sentenced to torture and then death. Not far from here you can begin the Stations of the Cross at the Chapel of the Flagellation, a small but moving chapel recalling Jesus torture at the hands of the Romans.

The Stations of the Cross are located along the Via Dolorosa, the "way of suffering," which was developed sometime in the 1300s as a way of helping pilgrims walk in Jesus' footsteps and identify with their Lord. There are fourteen events that are recalled, some clearly described in the Bible, others attributed to church tradition. Small chapels and stone markers can be found at each station along the road. Ultimately this journey will lead you to Christianity's holiest place, Calvary, where Jesus was crucified, and the tomb where Jesus was laid to rest. Both of these places are found within the walls of the Church of the Holy Sepulcher. Though elements of the stations and even places within the Church of the Holy Sepulcher are not found within Scripture and date far later than the time of Christ, there is a strong likelihood that Christ was actually crucified and buried in the area covered by, or near, the church. This place is holy ground.

In the video that is available to accompany this book, I take the viewer to these places. For a more in-depth look, see my book and video *24 Hours That Changed the World.*

Jesus, on the other hand, had no soldiers. He led a ragtag band of followers who waved palm branches as he passed by on a donkey. Wisam Salsaa, a modern-day Palestinian artisan, historian, and guide, describes Jesus' parade as history's first nonviolent demonstration. This demonstration was for a king and kingdom built upon a radical desire to love God and a commitment to love one's enemies.

As Jesus rode the donkey down the Mount of Olives, he looked out over Jerusalem and began to weep. The only other time in the Gospels that we read about Jesus weeping was when his friend Lazarus died. Now he wept over the city, saying to Jerusalem:

If you, even you, had only recognized on this day the things that make for peace! But now they are hidden from your eyes. Indeed, the days will come upon you, when your enemies will set up ramparts around you and surround you, and hem you in on every side. They will crush you to the ground, you and your children within you, and they will not leave within you one stone upon another; because you did not recognize the time of your visitation from God. (Luke 19:42-44 NRSV)

Jesus knew that despite the cheering crowds he would soon be rejected as King although this was not why he wept. He knew that as the crowds rejected him, they would be rejecting his way. They would reject his call to love their enemies, to pray for those who persecuted, and to do good to those who did wrong. They would instead choose to follow the way of the sword. Eventually the people of Jerusalem would rally behind two would-be messiahs who in A.D. 66 would lead a revolt against Rome. In response, Rome would send sixty thousand troops to crush the revolt, slaughtering a million Jews. The Romans would burn the Temple and the Holy City, just as Jesus foresaw.

Jesus' response in the face of oppression was mirrored two millennia later in the words and actions of the Rev. Martin Luther King, Jr., who said, in effect, "You can bomb our homes and threaten our children and hurt us, but we will wear you down by our capacity to suffer. And we will love you. We will love you until that day comes when finally we win you over. When we do, we'll have a double victory, for you will be changed and our world will be changed."[15]

When I was in Israel researching this book, the top story on America's nightly news was whether Israel would bomb preemptively Iran's nuclear facilities. I watched as Iran's leaders warned that if Israel struck them, they would be striking Israel in return. I began to wonder where the nearest bomb shelters were. In the midst of these threats that could destroy tens of thousands of people, an Israeli man named Ronny Edry started a campaign on Facebook to change the dialogue. The Facebook page was called "Israel Loves Iran." Edry invited Israelis to use the page to express their concern for Iranians and their rejection of war. Quickly thousands of Israelis began expressing their concern for Iran and their desire for peace. Soon Iranians picked up the ball, launching an "Iran Loves Israel" page. To most

Destruction of the Temple

In A.D. 66, tensions between Jews and Romans erupted into outright rebellion against Rome. The ensuing three years would see both a civil war among the Jews and a war against the Romans. Rome responded to the rebellion by sending as many as 60,000 well-trained and armed soldiers who systematically crushed any elements of the rebellion in the north and along the coast before turning their attention to Jerusalem. By the end of July, A.D. 70, the Romans had penetrated the city walls and slaughtered as many as a million Jews. After plundering the Temple, the Romans tore down its walls and burned it to the ground, just as Jesus had foreseen.

Among the most fascinating things to see in Jerusalem is a first-century street that runs along the western wall of the Temple Mount, just south of the place where Jews come to pray at the wall. This area is part of the Jerusalem Archaeological Park and the Davidson Center. From this street one can see the remains of shops that lined the street in the time of Jesus. What is really astounding, though, is the pile of huge stones that were cast down by the Romans when they destroyed the Temple. The stones have been lying in their current position for nearly two thousand years, a silent testimony to the destruction of Jerusalem foretold by Jesus on Palm Sunday.

people the idea seemed naïve, even silly, but it struck me as consistent with the absurd ways of Jesus, who urged his followers to defeat violence and aggression with love.

On Palm Sunday, Jesus wept because the people of Jerusalem did not embrace the "things that make for peace." Swords would bring, not freedom, but catastrophic destruction.

What kind of King is Jesus? He is a King who wanted his people to love their enemies and who promised that the peacemakers would be blessed.

Monday:
The Cleansing of the Temple

Mark tells us that Jesus made his way to the Temple on Monday. (Matthew and Luke place this on Sunday.) There, in the Court of the Gentiles, Jesus found merchants and money changers. Worshipers at the Temple were required to trade their normal currency for Temple Shekels. The exchange rates favored the money changers. Likewise, Temple worship involved animal sacrifices, and the lambs or pigeons used had to be without blemish. The merchants sold animals that were certified to be acceptable, but at vastly inflated prices. Both schemes enriched the merchants and the high priest.

Jesus, seeing that the poor were being ripped off in the name of God, became incensed. He overturned the money changers' tables and threw them out of the Temple, quoting Jeremiah in saying they had made the Temple a "den of thieves." Seldom do we find Jesus angry in the Gospels, but when Jesus is angry it is always at hypocrisy in the name of religion.

In his own temptations Jesus was offered all the wealth and power a man could want if he would lay aside his convictions and the cross, but he refused. He spoke on numerous occasions about the choice we have as human beings to serve God or money. Religious leaders and organizations are not immune to this temptation and, should they choose to worship money, they can manipulate and misuse their power to take advantage of their people. This is still a problem today, which is why accountability is important in religious organizations and why religious leaders must be cognizant of this temptation and guard against it. It is easy to point out the sins of others, such as fallen televangelists and prosperity preachers who promised answered prayers and wealth to those who would send a check. But all of us struggle with the temptations surrounding money and the place of material possessions in our lives.

When Jesus "cleansed the Temple," he sealed his fate. He had disrupted business on the most lucrative week of the year—the ancient equivalent of closing down a shopping mall the week before Christmas. As long as Jesus was in Jerusalem, the merchants were losing money, and so were the high priest and his cronies, who likely received some portion of the merchants' revenue. From this time on, the religious leaders were looking for a way to discredit Jesus, or to do away with him entirely.

What kind of King is Jesus? He is a King who refused to allow people to be taken advantage of, particularly by those who did so in the name of God.

Tuesday:
Continuing Confrontations with Religious Leaders

On Tuesday Jesus entered the Temple courts once more and began to teach.[16] As the people gathered around him, the chief priests and elders came and asked him, "By what authority are you doing these things, and who gave you that authority?" Imagine! They asked the Son of God by what authority he came into his Father's house to teach, heal, and cast out the vendors!

At that point, Jesus began telling parables directed at the religious leaders. He didn't pull any punches, since he knew that his fate already had been sealed. His words were meant to penetrate the blindness of the leaders. The crowds listen in stunned amazement.

Jesus said to the religious leaders, "There was a man who had two sons. He told his first son to go work in the vineyard, but the son refused. Later the son changed his mind and went to work as his father had asked. The father then told his second son to go work in the vineyard, and the son agreed to go. But the son did not do as he had promised. Which of the two sons did his father's will?"

The religious leaders replied, "The first son." Jesus replied, "Yes, and I tell you, the tax collectors and prostitutes will enter the kingdom of God ahead of you."

You could hear the crowd gasp. They knew what Jesus was saying—that the religious leaders had promised to do God's work but had not done it; while the "sinners" had rejected God's call at first, but then under Jesus' ministry had chosen to live as a part of God's kingdom. The parable echoes through history. How many times have we claimed to follow Christ but then refused to do what he asks of us? And how many times have we seen those who apparently have rejected Christ nevertheless live according to his words?

Jesus' parables then became even more pointed, foretelling Jesus' own death at the hands of the religious leaders and the judgment that would come down upon them, and those they led, if they refused to heed his call.

After hearing his pointed parables, the religious leaders sought to trap Jesus in his words. They asked questions meant to lead him to say something for which he could be charged, or which at the very least would alienate the crowds. It was in the context of their questioning that Jesus offered the two great commands: "Love the Lord your God with all your heart and with all your soul and with all your mind" and "Love your neighbor as yourself." These two commands summarize the essence of the Christian life.

Finally Jesus addressed the crowd and his disciples in the most direct way possible, speaking about the sins of the Pharisees and the teachers of the Law (see Matthew 23). Jesus described the religious leaders as those who "do not practice what they preach." He repeatedly called them hypocrites. The Greek word *hypokrites* was used to describe an actor on a stage; in other words, Jesus was accusing them of being pretenders. He went on to call them "snakes" and a "brood of vipers" (Matthew 23:33 NIV). Once again we can feel the anger of Christ at the way in which the religious leaders had missed the point.

I wonder if you ever feel like a pretender in your faith? Every pastor has known the feeling of being an actor on stage when it comes to faith. All of us, like the Pharisees, have sometimes been "whitewashed tombs"—beautiful on the outside but filled with decay on the inside.

What kind of King is Jesus? He is a King who condemned hypocrisy and commanded us to love.

Wednesday:
Parables of the Last Judgment

In Matthew 24:1, Jesus left the Temple and continued his teaching on the Mount of Olives. There is a tragic symbolism here. Jesus, the very incarnation of God, had come to the Temple, the house of the Lord, and the people in charge of the house did not recognize him. Now, in a way that no one but Jesus could have comprehended, the glory of the Lord left the Temple and no one really noticed.

Once Jesus left the Temple, he spoke again about the judgment to come upon Jerusalem.[17] When the disciples commented on the magnificent buildings of the Temple, Jesus responded, "I tell you the truth, not one stone here will be left on another. Every one will be thrown down" (Matthew 24:2 NIV).

Jesus and his disciples walked through the Kidron Valley and up to the Mount of Olives, where they had a panoramic view of the Temple. The disciples asked, "When will this destruction occur, and what will be the sign of your coming and of the end of the ages?"

What follows in Matthew 24 is often seen as a road map for the second coming of Christ and the "end times." But much of what we read in that chapter is Jesus' response to the disciples' question about when the Temple would be destroyed, which would occur in A.D. 70. The genius of Jesus' words in Matthew 24, what scholars call the "little Apocalypse," is that in those words every generation can see their own times. And no matter what those times are, the message is the same: "Therefore keep watch, because you do not know on what day your Lord will come" (Matthew 24:42 NIV). We are called to be ready at all times for the return of Christ.

Some Christians devote a great deal of their energy to the Second Coming of Christ. Some predict dates, develop detailed charts, or find themselves seeking to discern the "signs of the times." But only a small portion of Jesus' teaching described the events surrounding his return. What he did describe was not meant to lead us to elaborate theories of his return, but to encourage us to live differently, vigilantly, faithfully, and hopefully because we know that one day he will return.

The end of Matthew 24 and all of Matthew 25 are made up of four parables about what it means to be ready for Christ's return. In the first parable, Matthew 24:45-51, Jesus spoke of a servant left in charge of a house while the master was away. The servant's task was to feed the other servants at the appropriate times. *Being ready meant taking care of the other servants as the master of the house commanded.*

Jesus followed this immediately with a second parable, about ten bridesmaids preparing to escort a bridegroom to a wedding banquet. (Remember, Jesus had spoken of a wedding banquet in 22:1 and following.) The bridegroom was delayed, during which time the five poorly prepared bridesmaids ran out of oil for their lamps. While they were away trying to purchase oil, the bridegroom returned and proceeded to the wedding banquet with the five bridesmaids whose lamps were full of oil and were ready for the bridegroom's return.

The parable is an allegory, and it is possible that the oil and lamps represent faith that is manifest in good deeds. Earlier in the Gospel Jesus had said, "You are the light of the world. No one lights a lamp and covers it under a basket. Let your light so shine before others that they might see your good works and give glory to your Father in heaven." If Jesus intended this connection, *then being ready for the coming of the King may mean trusting him and doing his work.*

Matthew records a third parable, in which a man went away on a long journey, but before doing so he divided up his wealth among three of his servants, giving one servant five talents, another servant two talents, and a third servant one talent.[18] The servants were expected to use the talents and to multiply them on behalf of the master—in other words, they were to act as investment managers. Two of the servants multiplied the master's investment, and one buried it.

Was Jesus interested in making money? No. This story was another way of telling the parable of the soils and the sower.

Each of us has been given so much time, influence, blessings. Do we hide it, preserve it, keep it safe? Or do we give it away, multiply it, use it to expand the Kingdom? *Being ready for the King's coming, according to this parable, is about faithfully using the resources the King has given you for his purposes.*

Often at funerals I have quoted the master's words to the faithful servants: "Well done, good and faithful servant. Enter into your rest." Oh, to hear those words on the day we meet Christ face to face! The parable reminds us that our lives, resources, strengths, and blessings are all given to us with expectations that we will use them for God's glory in expanding his kingdom.

I think of Fred Ball, a grocer who was a part of the congregation I serve. His family started a small grocery operation. Fred's father, and later Fred himself, expanded the business, developing innovative grocery stores with ideas that were adopted by other grocers across the country. But Fred never forgot that everything he had was simply on loan, and that he held it as a sacred trust. When there was need, he always helped. He saw his employees as people whose care he was entrusted with. He wanted his stores to bless others. Seeking to live his life as God's servant, he was always generous toward others and toward God. He was very successful as a grocer, but he carried his success with humility. I was blessed to preach at his funeral last year. It was easy to say with confidence that on the day of his passing, Fred heard the words of the master saying, "Well done, good and faithful servant."

In the fourth and last of Jesus' parables reported here by Matthew, Jesus brought into the open what he had hinted at in the first three parables. He noted that at the final judgment, those who would be blessed with eternal life are those who, while walking on this earth, fed the hungry, gave drink to the thirsty, welcomed the stranger, clothed the naked, cared for the sick, and visited the prisoner. *This is what it means to be ready for the King's coming.*

All that Jesus said in Matthew 24 and 25 was meant to lead his hearers, and modern-day readers, to ask, "Am I ready to meet my King?" For none of us knows the day or the hour when we will stand before him.

After telling the four parables, Jesus ate supper in the home of a leper. There, a prostitute came and poured out expensive scented oil upon his head, anointing him as King.[19] This is a profoundly beautiful reminder of Jesus' love for the outcasts.

What kind of King is Jesus? He is a King who chose to eat one of his final meals with an unclean leper and who was anointed by a prostitute.

Thursday:
Washing Feet and a Garden Prayer

On Thursday, as the lambs were being slaughtered and prepared for the Passover Seder, which is the Jewish meal commemorating God's deliverance of the Israelites from slavery in Egypt, Jesus sent two of his disciples to prepare the meal. He instructed them to do this in an upper room in Jerusalem. Meanwhile Jesus and the other disciples presumably spent the day together on the Mount of Olives.

When evening came, Jesus and his disciples entered the upstairs room and there recounted the story of the Exodus from Egypt. Ordinarily the meal would have been a joyous occasion celebrating the defining story of the Jewish people, but on this night Jesus redefined the story. After giving thanks for the unleavened bread, he presented it to his disciples and said, "Take and eat, this is my body given for you." The statement echoed his words two years earlier, when he had fed the multitudes: "I am the bread of life. Whoever comes to me will never go hungry" (John 6:35 NIV). Next, Jesus took the cup of wine, one of several that are shared at the Seder, and he said, "This is my blood of the covenant, which is poured out for many for the forgiveness of sins" (Matthew 26:28 NIV). When Jesus blessed the bread and wine that night, the disciples may have been confused by his words, which ultimately made sense only after his crucifixion and resurrection, when their meaning became clear.

The Passover meal has been observed by Jews for over three thousand years. In sharing this meal, they are taken back to the night when the Israelites finally were set free from slavery. They eat the same meal the Israelites ate on that night, and they celebrate salvation and deliverance at God's hand. This is their defining story. Jesus, in transforming the Passover meal, gave us a way in which we can be taken back to that night in the upper room. We join with Jesus in the meal. We remember his sacrificial death for us. The very act of eating this meal, of taking the bread and wine, is a way of saying, "Yes, Lord. I need you. I choose you. I accept you into my life. I find in you my strength and salvation." This meal becomes the Christian's defining story—a way of joining with Jesus and tangibly receiving him as one eats the bread and drinks the wine.

When the disciples had entered the upper room, they had walked past a pitcher of water and a towel that had been left by the owner of the house so they could wash their feet, a common custom at the time. When servants were present, it was their job to wash the guests' feet. In the absence of servants, the guests could wash their own feet. Each of the disciples had walked right past the pitcher and towel when they had come into the room. I have always suspected they passed the basin because they were afraid that if any one of them stopped, they would be expected to wash the feet of the others.

On this night some of the disciples, still thinking that Jesus was about to seize power in Jerusalem, were debating which one of them was "the greatest" (Luke 22:24). Jesus said to them, "The way of the world is to seek greatness—to have servants who serve you and to exercise authority over others. But that is not what you are to be like. The greatest among you must take the role of the least, and the one who rules should act as one who serves" (Luke 22:24-27, paraphrase).

John tells us that at this point Jesus got up from the table and retrieved the pitcher and towel. The disciples watched, shifting uncomfortably. Which one of them would he assign to wash the others' feet? To their amazement, Jesus got down on one knee and began to do it himself!

Long before the business world discovered "servant leadership," Jesus knew all about it. He demonstrated it that night when he washed his disciples feet. He demonstrated it the next day when he was crucified.

Jesus showed us that if we are constantly focused on ourselves, seeking to be served, we will find that we are never satisfied. But if we bless and serve others, carry our success with humility, understand and live the lesson he taught that night, we will find satisfaction, and often success, that we never anticipated.

After the supper was over, Jesus led his disciples from the upper city on Mt. Zion back through the Kidron Valley and to the Garden of Gethsemane on the opposite side of the valley. It was there, late into the night, that Jesus asked his disciples to pray for him. He went a stone's throw beyond them and there began to pray in anguish before God: "Father take this cup from me, yet not my will but thy will be done" (Mark 14:35, paraphrase).

I believe the scene is meant to remind us of the time in another garden, Eden, when Adam and Eve were being tempted to eat the forbidden fruit. As they stood before the Tree of the Knowledge of Good and Evil, their prayer was, in essence, "Not Thy will, but my will be done." Here, in this garden, Jesus was faced with the choice of fleeing for his own salvation or staying to die for the world. He prayed a very different prayer from Adam and Eve. His prayer was, "Not my will, but Thy will be done." In saying those words, he began the process of reversing Adam and Eve's curse. He began the work of restoring paradise.

As Jesus prayed, Judas arrived with a band of guards from the Temple. Judas betrayed Jesus with a kiss. The soldiers seized Jesus. The disciples fled. Jesus was bound and taken back to the upper city, to the home of Caiaphas, the high priest. There the Sanhedrin, the Jewish ruling council, had hastily been called together by night, a kangaroo court that could rule on Jesus' fate while the crowds were sleeping. Jesus was tried and found guilty of blasphemy. Outside, in the courtyard, Simon Peter thrice denied that he was one of Jesus' disciples.

What kind of King is Jesus? He is a King who saw himself as a servant willing to suffer for his people.[20]

Friday:
A Crucified King

Early on Friday morning, Jesus was taken to the Fortress Antonia, where he was brought before Pontius Pilate, the Roman governor of Judea and the guarantor of Roman justice. Though Pilate found no grounds for crucifying Jesus, his desire to please the Jewish leaders led him to sentence Jesus to death by crucifixion.

The soldiers, wishing to make an example of anyone who claimed to be a messiah, stripped Jesus, mocked him, beat him, and placed a crown of thorns upon his brow. This was the only crown our King ever wore when he walked on this earth. Yet somehow, as we imagine his cruel coronation, we see its glory—a King suffering for his people, laying down his life to ransom them.

After the soldiers had scourged and sought to dehumanize him, they led Jesus outside the city gates. The place of crucifixion was perhaps a half-mile from where his sentence was passed, and though his body had been abused, Jesus was forced to carry his cross to Calvary. When his body could no longer bear the 75-pound cross beam, a man named Simon of Cyrene was ordered by the Romans to carry Jesus' cross the rest of the way to the place of crucifixion.

The soldiers assembled the cross, then affixed a sign to the top indicating Jesus' crime and mocking him: "Jesus of Nazareth, King of the Jews." The soldiers laid Jesus on the cross and drove spikes through his wrists and ankles. They hoisted the cross into the air and settled its base into a hole so it would stand upright. There, still wearing the crown of thorns, Jesus hung for six hours, slowly dying.

This is the kind of King we follow, a King whose standard is the cross. Many look at the cross and see Christ's suffering and death for them, a "full and perfect sacrifice for the sins of the world," and indeed this is one of the profound and powerful truths of the cross. But there is more. When I look at the cross, I see a divine love story centered on a God who suffered to save the human race. This love is selfless and sacrificial, a parent dying for a child, a lover dying for the beloved. Ultimately, the cross is a sign of the lengths to which God will go to save us from our sin and brokenness. It reminds us that forgiveness came at a great price. Luke includes the words Jesus prayed from the cross, words that I find utterly astounding, a prayer transcending space and time, offered on Calvary for all people everywhere: "Father, forgive them, for they do not know what they are doing" (23:34 NIV).

When I look at the cross, I also see a mirror held up to our souls. Just as the story of Adam and Eve is archetypal—each of us hears the whisper of the serpent and at times succumbs—so too the story of the cross is our story. It is an indictment of the human race. We all like sheep have gone astray. Something in us is broken, and that brokenness was seen so clearly on the day when the religious leaders failed to see their own Messiah and instead insisted on his crucifixion. So when I look at the cross, it reminds me of all the things inside myself that I don't like to admit are there, all the ways I've betrayed and denied Christ or hurt other people, all that is in need of redemption and grace.

The cross leads me to gratitude and awe. It leads me to a love of Christ and a deep desire to follow him and live for him. I want to walk in his footsteps. I want to live as a citizen of his kingdom. I want to love as he loved. I want to practice his way.

What kind of King is Jesus? He is a King who rode into Jerusalem on a donkey, was anointed by a prostitute, was crowned with thorns, and was enthroned when he hung on a cross, so that you and I might know the love and mercy of God, accept it, and follow him.

Jesus' way calls for authentic followers, not religious hypocrites. His is a way that requires compassion for the hungry and thirsty and naked. Jesus' way is a path of servanthood and sacrificial love. And ultimately, walking in his footsteps will require us to "take up our cross" and follow him.

Reflection
What If Judas Had Waited?

> When Judas, his betrayer, saw that Jesus was condemned,
> he repented and brought back the thirty pieces of silver to
> the chief priests and the elders. He said, "I have sinned by
> betraying innocent blood." But they said, "What is that to us?
> See to it yourself." Throwing down the pieces of silver in the
> temple, he departed; and he went and hanged himself.
>
> (Matthew 27:3-5 NRSV)

Several years ago I had the chance to visit the place
tradition says Judas hung himself. The field, known as
Potter's Field or the Field of Blood, overlooks the Valley
of Hinnom—Gehenna. Gehenna served as the city trash
dump in the time of Christ and, owing to the constant fires
that burned the rubbish there, came to be synonymous
with hell. On the site of this field are the ruins of a twelfth-
century Crusader church and a host of discarded tombs in
the side of the rock outcropping. And there, in the middle
of the field, is a lone tree, a reminder that when Judas came
to this place, overwhelmed with guilt over having betrayed
Christ, he hanged himself.

As I stood at the tree, a thought came to me: "What if
Judas had waited three days?"

Many people, at some point, think of ending their lives. For most, the thought is momentary and fleeting. For others, who are overwhelmed by guilt, depression, or pain, the thought lingers. Tragically, a few will conclude that death offers the only way out.

Judas was one of these few. He had betrayed Christ. His friend would die for his betrayal. He felt there was no other way out. Yet I could not stop thinking, "If only he had waited three days." Had he waited, he would have seen Christ risen from the grave. He would have known that even his betrayal was not the final word. He could have fallen at Jesus' feet and cried out, "Lord, forgive me!" And what do you think Jesus would have said to Judas? Can there be any doubt that Jesus would have shown mercy to him?

Imagine what would have become of Judas had he waited. His witness might have been the most powerful of all the disciples'. Can you imagine him telling his story throughout the empire? "I betrayed the Lord for thirty pieces of silver. I watched him die on the cross. But on the third day, he rose. And he forgave even me! If he forgave me, what can he do for you?"

In our lives, we have moments that seem overwhelmingly bleak. We make a mess of things and see no way out. Judas felt that way. But the message of the cross and Resurrection is that God is the Lord of second chances. In even the most dire circumstances, there is always hope. After our most egregious sins, there is the offer of grace. In the darkest of times, there is an Easter yet to come.

Listen carefully: there is always hope. God is able to take the pain and despair of the present and bring from it something remarkable. You can't imagine it now, but look for someone or something that can help you find hope: a pastor, a family member, a friend, a suicide hotline. Remember Judas's story. Think about what could have been, if only he had waited three days.

Lord, help me to trust you in my darkest hour. Help me to remember that you can take something as ugly as a cross and turn it into an instrument of salvation. Grant me courage to keep walking when I feel like giving up. Amen.

* * *

If you or someone you know is struggling with suicidal thoughts, contact a suicide hotline in your area and contact the pastor of your local church.

From *The Way: 40 Days of Reflection*. Abingdon Press, 2012.

Travel Photos

Mount of Olives

Muslim Dome of the Rock, on Temple Mount

Kidron Valley

Temple in Jerusalem, destroyed by Rome in A.D. 66

Garden of Gethsemane

Via Dolorosa

St. Peter Galicantu, traditional site of Jesus' trial and Peter's denial

Peter denies Jesus three times "before the rooster crows twice" (Mark 14:30)

Epilogue
Your Defining Story

When it was evening on that day, the first day of the week, and the doors of the house where the disciples had met were locked for fear of the Jews, Jesus came and stood among them and said, "Peace be with you." After he said this, he showed them his hands and his side. Then the disciples rejoiced when they saw the Lord. Jesus said to them again, "Peace be with you. As the Father has sent me, so I send you." When he had said this, he breathed on them and said to them, "Receive the Holy Spirit. If you forgive the sins of any, they are forgiven them; if you retain the sins of any, they are retained."

John 20:19-23 NRSV

WHAT IS YOUR DEFINING STORY? What is the narrative that shapes the way you view the world and your place in it? What determines how you understand your life mission and ultimate destination, how you face adversity, and how you put into context all the suffering you see around you?

Now that we have followed Jesus through his ministry and the last week of his life, culminating in his death on the cross, we want to reflect on Easter—the climax of the defining story of the Christian faith. It is the event that shapes how we see the world.

On Thursday of his final week, Jesus was betrayed by one of his friends, arrested by the religious authorities, and found guilty of blasphemy for claiming to be the Son of God and the Jewish Messiah. On Friday he was sentenced to death by the Roman governor and crucified between two criminals, enduring hours of horrible pain and suffering before finally breathing his last. He was taken down from the cross, hastily prepared for burial, and placed in a borrowed tomb, which then had a large stone rolled in front of it.

As far as anyone could see, that was that. It was over. The disciples who had been with Jesus for three years were in hiding, for fear that they would be arrested and crucified themselves.

Friday Was Not the End of the Story

On Saturday of Holy Week, Jesus was dead and the disciples had gone into hiding. What would it take for this frightened, grief-stricken, and dispirited group to rebound from that dark place and to go on after the arrest, trial, and execution of the man they thought would be the Messiah? It's clear that if our defining story had ended with Jesus' burial, today there might not be a Christian faith. But early on Sunday morning, the women

The Church of the Holy Sepulcher

Though some suggest that Christ was crucified and buried at a place called Gordon's Calvary, the earliest Christian witnesses place Calvary and Christ's burial at the site where the Church of the Holy Sepulcher is located. The first church was built on the site in the fourth century, though Christians made pilgrimage there beginning as early as the second century. That first church was destroyed in 1009 by a Muslim caliph hostile to the Christian faith, but after his death the church was rebuilt with the permission of the next caliph. Remnants of the first church still can be seen on the site.

The exterior of the church is unimpressive and a bit unkempt. The fact that the building is claimed by several different factions of the Christian faith, along with disagreements among these factions, has affected the restoration and repair of the building.

I'll walk you through the building in the order in which it should be experienced. (I've followed this order in the video available with this study.) Immediately upon coming through the main entrance, turn to the right and climb a set of stairs. At the top of the stairs is what is left of the rocky hill called Calvary, where Jesus was crucified between two thieves. The first chapel you will come to is the Catholic chapel of the Calvary. The chapel is simple. It includes a powerful mosaic showing the crucified Christ with a Roman soldier, Mary Magdalene, and Mary the mother of Jesus. Take the time to absorb this and other mosaics around you.

After spending a few moments in the chapel, follow the crowd to the left, where you will come to the Orthodox chapel of the Crucifixion, built on the rock hilltop over the place where tradition says Jesus was crucified. This is Christianity's holiest place. This space, covered with brass lamps and icons, is often crowded, jarring the Western sensibilities of many Protestants. I encourage visitors to look past the crowd, the icons, and the brass lamps, and to focus instead on the significance of the place. A central altar is built over the center of the rocky hilltop. On either side of the altar is a glass case, where you can see the hilltop and the location where the thieves were crucified beside Jesus. Pilgrims kneel and crawl under the altar to put their hands inside an opening where they can touch the top of Calvary, connecting for a moment with the very place where church tradition says Jesus was crucified.

Whether this was the exact location or not, the act of touching the stone and praying has always been very meaningful to me.

After exiting the chapel, you'll descend another set of stairs and come to the "stone of unction," a late addition to the Church of the Holy Sepulcher. It is unlikely that this is the place where Christ's body was prepared for burial, as some have said, but as a symbol of that place it is powerful. Christians kneel, touch the stone, and pray. The beautiful tile mosaics above the stone tell the story of Christ's crucifixion, preparation for burial, and interment.

Head to the right, back in the direction you came from, and you'll have an opportunity to tour the rest of this very old church. As you descend a set of stairs, you'll see more chapels and a lower cistern, where tradition says that in the 300s, Saint Helena found the cross of Christ—a tradition I find unlikely, but interesting nonetheless. Coming back up the stairs and continuing around the building to the right, you'll pass a number of other chapels, including one that purports to be where prisoners were held awaiting their crucifixion.

Finally, you'll pass a series of giant columns, some of which may date back to the fourth-century church, and you'll come to the rotunda. In the center of this space is the Edicule, a building constructed around the tomb of Christ. Long lines form as pilgrims wait to pray inside this small building, at the very site where tradition says Christ was raised to life.

The crowds and the centuries of additions sometimes make it hard for Christians to appreciate the Church of the Holy Sepulcher, but if you can set aside these distractions when you enter and focus on the story, you'll find it to be a powerful space.

who followed Jesus went to the tomb and found that the stone had been rolled away.

What had happened? What did it mean? Their first thought was that someone had stolen Jesus' body.

Shortly after the women arrived and found the empty tomb, Jesus appeared to them and said, "Look, I'm here. It's me. Touch me. Tell my disciples I'm alive." Later that day he appeared to the disciples, and that appearance changed everything. The message was clear: Neither sin, nor hate, nor evil, nor even death would have the final word. God, in raising Jesus from the dead, was shouting to the human race: *Love has conquered hate, grace has conquered sin, hope has conquered despair, and life has conquered death!* Love, grace, hope, life—these have the final word because of Christ's resurrection. That is our defining story as Christians.

Last year, LaVon and I traveled to northern Europe, where I'd been invited by the Bishop of the Scandinavian countries to speak at a conference for Methodist pastors and leaders. This part of the world is sometimes described as "post-Christian." There are churches everywhere—Christianity is still part of the culture—but very few people attend them. We had a free evening in Copenhagen and it was raining, so we decided to go see a movie. One of the few shows in English was *Harry Potter and the Deathly Hallows,* and we went in to see it. I had not seen any of the Harry Potter movies—I wasn't against them, just hadn't seen them—nor had I read any of the books, though I knew a little bit about the story.

About three-quarters of the way through the movie, it hit me how familiar the plot seemed. And then I realized, *I know this story!* A young man lays down his life to save his friends. He appears to be dead. All seems lost. And then he opens his eyes, defeats his arch enemy, and restores hope!

As I watched the film, I also watched the audience, and that was an amazing experience. In Scandinavia, 95 percent of the population—nineteen out of twenty people—don't go to church. Those were the people sitting all around me. As Harry went forward to give up his life for his friends, I could hear people crying. When Harry rose, they cheered. And when he finally defeated Voldemort, they broke out in joyful applause.

I don't think they were cheering just for the fictional Harry Potter. They were cheering for the idea that life conquers death, that good conquers evil, that evil will never have the final word. That idea was best demonstrated not in a movie, but in Jerusalem two thousand years ago. Jesus gave himself to save the world, so that death and evil would not triumph. He was crucified, dead, and buried, but on the third day he rose from the grave. Ultimately, as the Bible proclaims in the Revelation of John, Christ will defeat the forces of evil.

There's not a human being alive who doesn't secretly yearn for the truth conveyed in our defining story.

Every year I go through my library and look for classic books from great preachers of previous generations to see how they approached Easter. Last year I pulled down from the shelf *Sangster's Special-Day Sermons.*

William Sangster was pastor at the largest Methodist church in England during World War II and for ten years after that. He had a passion for helping thinking people know Christ, and for renewing the Methodist Church, which had been in decline in England for fifty years. He also wrote numerous books. *Sangster's Special-Day Sermons* was his last.

Sangster's church, Westminster Methodist, sits across from Westminster Abbey, and its Methodist Central Hall seats about three thousand people. Every Sunday morning and evening, people would pack the place to hear Sangster preach. He was there as World War II kicked into high gear, including one stretch when the Nazis bombed London for fifty-seven straight nights. During the war, tens of thousands of people sought refuge at some point in the basement of Central Hall. Sangster and his wife would stay up until midnight helping people get settled in, and then they would sleep on the floor of the men's bathroom.

Every weekend, the church filled with people looking for a message that spoke to their heads and their hearts, something that could help them make sense of the evil in their world and let them find hope in the midst of it. Week after week, he reminded them of our defining story—that this is not a world without suffering but a world in which God has come to us, to walk with us and promise that evil will never have the final word.

After the war, Sangster's church became the first home of the United Nations before it moved to New York City. Then, in 1956, at the age of 56, Sangster was diagnosed with Lou Gehrig's Disease, or ALS. Within a year he couldn't preach anymore and had to surrender his pulpit. A year later, he was unable to speak. Before his death in 1960, he decided to put together one last book of sermons—the one I had taken down from the shelf.

William Sangster's Easter sermon was quite good, but it was the foreword to the book, written by his son Paul, which moved me to tears:

> These sermons form the last work [of my dad].... They were sent to the publisher only a day or two before he died....The last weeks of his life...he was virtually helpless, retaining only a little strength in two fingers of his right hand with which to hold a pen. His voice had long been lost, and his only means of communication left...was his pen—and therefore, this book....Yet the finest sermon he ever preached is not in this collection, though the book tells something of it. That distinction belongs not to any he preached from the pulpit nor to any printed word, but to the last years of his life. It was then that [my dad] preached his best and preached, curiously enough, in silence.[21]

Sangster's defining story was the cross and resurrection of Jesus Christ. In the midst of his battle with Lou Gehrig's Disease, he believed not that God afflicted him, but that God was with him every single day, and that somehow God could use even this for his glory. He believed that in the end, life conquers death and so disease would not have the final word.

That is what a life looks like whose defining story is the cross and resurrection of Jesus Christ. Sangster's story is a story of victory and hope—a living out of Christ's crucifixion and resurrection.

I have been the senior pastor of the Church of the Resurrection for over two decades. Every year I end my Easter sermon the same way. I mention that people ask me from time to time, "Do you really believe this stuff? You're a smart guy. Do you really believe that Jesus rose from the dead?"

My response is always the same: "I not only believe it; I'm counting on it."

I'm counting on the fact that there is always hope. I'm counting on the fact that God walks with us through hell and back again. I'm counting on the fact that God forgives our sins and that he's the God of the second chance. I'm counting on the fact that ultimately we don't have to be afraid. I'm counting on the fact that sin and hate and sickness and death will not have the final word. When we walk in the footsteps of the resurrected Christ, we walk with hope.

Sangster counted on it. Peter and the disciples counted on it. What are you counting on? What is your defining story?

Reflection
Some Doubted

> But Thomas (who was called the Twin), one of the twelve,
> was not with them when Jesus came. So the other disciples
> told him, "We have seen the Lord." But he said to them,
> "Unless I see the mark of the nails in his hands, and put my
> finger in the mark of the nails and my hand in his side, I
> will not believe." (John 20:24-25 NRSV)

Michael was a guide on my first trip to Israel. He was
Jewish, but it was obvious he knew more about Jesus than
the average Christian. As Michael described the various
places we went, he assumed more New Testament knowledge than some of our people had, and I would have to stop
and explain what he had just said. Michael was more like a
professor of New Testament than a Holy Land guide.

At one point, away from the rest of my group, I asked
him, "Michael, you genuinely seem to love Jesus, yet you
are not a Christian. Tell me about this." He said, "I do love
him. I love what he taught. I love what he did. I love the way
he cared for the sick and the broken. I grieve the tragedy
of his death and believe he gave his life to demonstrate the
path of love, and to show God's love." I said, "Michael, it
sounds like you are a Christ-follower." He responded, "My
only problem is that I can't find the faith to believe in the
Resurrection."

Michael was not the first to struggle with the concept of Jesus' resurrection. In Luke's gospel, the women were the first to meet the risen Christ, but when they told the disciples that he was risen, "these words seemed to them an idle tale, and they did not believe them" (Luke 24:11 NRSV). When Jesus finally appeared to the disciples, Thomas was not with them, so he did not believe. In fact, *ten disciples* told him they had seen Christ risen, and still he refused to believe. His skepticism earned him the nickname "Doubting Thomas." Matthew, in his account, depicts the disciples seeing the resurrected Christ for the first time in Galilee when he gave the great commission. Matthew notes, "When they saw him, they worshiped him; but some doubted" (Matthew 28:17 NRSV).

I think Jesus had great empathy for doubters. He knew the Resurrection would be hard to believe, which is why, after appearing to Thomas he said, "Because you have seen me, you have believed; blessed are those who have not seen and yet believed" (John 20:29 NIV).

The first time I read Matthew and Mark's Gospels I was not yet a Christian. I, too, found the Resurrection difficult to believe. Finally, as I read Luke's account, it began to make sense. I asked myself, "What would be different if the Resurrection had not occurred?" Jesus would have died on the cross, just the same. But this death would be a defeat, not the prelude to a victory. Evil would have won. Hate, fear, and bigotry would have been the victors. The apostles would have returned to fishing. Paul would never have met the risen Christ. The Great Commission would never have been given. The great message of redemption, forgiveness, and hope would not be known throughout the world.

It finally hit me that the story *had* to end with the Resurrection if in fact it was God's story. Evil could not have the last word. Death could not have the final say. I came to trust that God, who called forth the universe through his creative power, also had the power to bring about Christ's resurrection from the grave. Realizing this, I came to trust that the tomb was empty and that the women, the disciples, and Paul had in fact seen the risen Christ.

God raised his son from the dead. I not only believe this, I'm counting on it. But I still have empathy for those, such as Michael, who struggle with doubt. I assured Michael that he was in good company—that the earliest disciples of Jesus struggled with the Resurrection, too. I invited him to keep following Jesus' way and to continue pondering the meaning of the Resurrection. I suggested that one day he, too, might come to see the logic, and power, of the Resurrection.

"Lord, I believe. Help thou my unbelief." Thank you for your patience with doubters such as Thomas. Help me to trust in the Easter story and to know that because you live, I will live also. Amen.

From *The Way: 40 Days of Reflection*. Abingdon Press, 2012.

Acknowledgments

MY DEEPEST APPRECIATION to Rob Webster, Michael Collins, and my wife LaVon Hamilton for traveling with me to the Holy Land to record the video that accompanies this study. Alex Schwindt filmed the studio footage and other U.S. footage and did the final edit on the video. Thanks, Alex! Great work!

I am also deeply grateful to Educational Opportunities Tours and its founder, James Ridgeway Sr., who provided transportation to the Holy land for this project. For more information on travel to the Holy Land, go to www.EO.TravelWithUs.com.

Special thanks to Ron Kidd, my very patient and gifted editor at Abingdon, and to Rob Simbeck, who took my sermon manuscripts and from them crafted the first draft of the book. I'm also appreciative of Phillip Francis for his work on the maps and Ken Strickland for his illustration.

Finally, I'd like to thank Susan Salley and the team of terrific people who have worked with her in making possible the trilogy of books and studies I've prepared on the life of Jesus.

Notes

1. A possible exception is the fact that Matthew tells us Mary, Joseph, and Jesus resided in Egypt until it was safe for them to return to the Holy Land. Though some have speculated about Jesus' age during the trip described in Luke 2, we actually have no solid evidence about it.
2. See http://www.thenazareneway.com/essene_and_christian_parallels. htm.
3. John was six months older than Jesus and began his ministry just before Jesus. Luke tells us that Jesus was about thirty when he began his ministry. Why thirty? In Numbers 4:2, God asked for a census of the Levites who were thirty and over so that they could serve in the Tent of Meeting (the precursor to the Temple), which would indicate that priests began their work at thirty. Perhaps more important, David became King of Israel at age thirty (2 Samuel 5:4).
4. For more information about the friars, to see a short video or to take a virtual tour through the site visit: http://www.capernaum.custodia.org.
5. It was common for multiple families to dwell in the same home and for these homes to be expanded when adult children married or when other kin needed a place to live.
6. As an example, lying and deception are wrong, yet consider the story of André Trocmé, who was pastor to the French village of Le Chambon-sur-Lignon during Hitler's regime. Trocmé led his people to save five thousand Jews from Nazi death camps through a system of lies and deception that risked the lives of every villager. It is a profound story of good.

7. I've heard many teach that the "eye of the needle" was a narrower gate within the larger gates in the city walls. If you can find first-century evidence of this, please write me. It is likely that centuries after the time of Christ, such smaller gates were used (I've seen them), but I've not found evidence that they existed by this name in the time of Jesus.

8. Most scholars believe that the Sermon on the Mount represents Matthew's collection of some of the ethical and practical teachings of Jesus, and that it was given in pieces, probably multiple times over his ministry, making Matthew's placement of it "on the mountain" an even clearer sign of the point he hopes to make about Jesus as the new Moses, and the Sermon on the Mount as the new law.

9. The Law of Moses in Deuteronomy 24:1ff allowed men to "send their wives away" with a certificate of divorce if the man found something "indecent" about her. No one was apparently clear, after the time of Moses, what constituted something "indecent"—it was not infidelity, which was covered by adultery. So the more liberal interpreters believed it had to do with anything a spouse (usually husband) found unpleasing about his mate.

10. Jesus added, "Except on the grounds of unchastity."

11. The New Revised Standard Version leaves out the word *so* or *therefore,* but it is present in the Greek and appears in the New International Version and the Common English Bible.

12. The "Navy Hymn" is also known as "Eternal Father, Strong to Save," originally written as a poem in 1860 by William Whiting, for a student who was about to sail for the United States. The melody, published in 1861, was composed by fellow Englishman Rev. John Bacchus Dykes, an Episcopalian clergyman.

13. From Martin Luther King, Jr.'s sermon of April 3, 1968, "I've Been to the Mountain Top," delivered at Bishop Charles Mason Temple, Memphis Tennessee.

14. Josephus, the first-century Jewish historian, noted that 250,000 lambs were slaughtered for the festival. Assuming one lamb for each family celebrating the Passover, the number of visitors could have been much higher.

15. Sermon by Martin Luther King, Jr., delivered Christmas, 1957, Dexter Avenue Baptist Church, Montgomery, Alabama.

16. The chronology of the things Jesus said and did on Holy Week may be debated. I've placed the cleansing of the Temple on Monday following Mark, but in the remainder of this chronology I am generally following Matthew's account, while drawing from elements in Luke and John.

17. I place this event and the teachings of Matthew 24 and 25 on Wednesday of Holy Week.

18. A talent was a unit of measure indicating weight and, when applied to precious metals, indicating monetary value. Its weight varied in different cultures but in Rome was about seventy pounds and in Israel perhaps more. Hence, one talent of silver or gold would have been a vast amount of money.

19. The story is told in several different ways in the Gospels. In John, it is Mary the sister of Lazarus who anointed Jesus. In Luke, the woman was a prostitute who came to the home of Simon the Pharisee. In Matthew and Mark, she is identified only as a woman who brought expensive perfume and poured it on his head.

20. For a much more detailed account of this night and of Good Friday, please see my book *24 Hours That Changed the World,* which devotes six chapters to the events beginning with the Last Supper and ending with Christ's burial, and also *Final Words,* about Jesus' final words from the cross.

21. From *Sangster's Special-Day Sermons,* by W.E. Sangster (Abingdon Press, 1961); page 5.

About the Author

ADAM HAMILTON is senior pastor of The United
Methodist Church of the Resurrection in the Kansas City
area with an average weekly attendance of over 10,000. It has
been cited as the most influential mainline church in America.
Hamilton speaks across the U.S. each year on leadership and
connecting with nonreligious and nominally religious people.
In 2013 the White House invited him to preach at the National
Prayer Service as part of the presidential inauguration festivities.
In 2016 he was appointed to the President's Advisory Council on
Faith-Based and Neighborhood Partnerships.

A master at explaining questions of faith in a down-to-
earth fashion, he is the author of many books including *The
Journey, The Way, 24 Hours That Changed the World, Enough,
Why: Making Sense of God's Will, When Christians Get it Wrong,
Seeing Gray in a World of Black and White, Forgiveness, Love to
Stay, Making Sense of the Bible,* and *Half Truths.* To learn more
about Adam and to follow his regular blog postings, visit www.
AdamHamilton.org.

CPSIA information can be obtained
at www.ICGtesting.com
Printed in the USA
FSHW020509280121
78102FS